Anti-Inflammatory Diet Cookbook for Beginners

A Guide With A Sample Meal Plan And Simple
Recipes To Help Your Immune System Rebuild
And Enjoy Healthy Food Every Day

Sebastian Young

Your Free Gift

As a way of saying thanks for your purchase, to our readers we

offer as a gift a printable recipe book, to download for free:

"Cookbook Journal",

a diary in which to keep track of all your culinary inventions,

assigning each one an evaluation, the difficulty of execution

and much more.

Click this link to free download https://dl.bookfunnel.com/i3sq7ljm6z

Tables of Contents

Chapter 5: Snacks Recipes

Chapter 1: Introduction to Anti-Inflammatory Diet

Before you can clearly understand why an anti-inflammatory diet may be beneficial and is now one of the most talked-about diets, you must first comprehend what inflammation is.

1.1 What is Inflammation?

When you hear the term "inflammation," you may think of the swelling and redness that occurs when you stub your toe. There are two obvious visible indicators of inflammation, but there's more to it than that.

Inflammation is a normal aspect of the immune system's response. Inflammatory cells are sent to the rescue when your body is defending against infection or injury. This causes swelling, redness, and discomfort, as well as other symptoms. That's very normal and understandable.

That is, as long as the body remains under control. When inflammation persists and does not go away completely the scenario changes. Chronic inflammation puts your body on high alert all of the time, and it may lead to serious health problems, including diabetes, Alzheimer's disease, heart disease and cancer.Fortunately, you have some influence over your inflammation levels. Inflammation may be increased by factors such as being overweight or obese, smoking and drinking excessively. Your diet also plays a major role, and some doctors believe that changing your diet and drinking habits rather than taking medicine is a better way to reduce inflammation. Taking chronic pain medicine only when absolutely necessary is also a smart idea since many medicines have unpleasant side effects, including sleepiness, fogginess and memory loss.

1.2 What Causes it?

Inflammation may be exacerbated by certain lifestyle variables, particularly those that are repeated. High-fructose corn syrup and Sugar are particularly dangerous when consumed in large quantities. Diabetes, insulin resistance and obesity are all possible outcomes.

Consuming a lot of refined carbohydrates, such as white bread, has also been linked to inflammation, obesity and insulin resistance, according to scientists.

Furthermore, trans fats found in processed and packaged meals have been proven to cause inflammation and damage to the endothelial cells that protect your arteries.

Another suspected reason is vegetable oils, which are found in many processed meals. Regular consumption may cause an omega-6 to omega-3 fatty acid imbalance, which some experts think promotes inflammation.

Excessive alcohol & processed meat consumption may also cause inflammation in the body. In addition, a lack of physical activity with a lot of sitting is a significant non-dietary component that may cause inflammation.

1.3 What is Anti-Inflammatory Diet?

Some foods include ingredients that might cause or exacerbate inflammation. Sugary or processed foods are more likely to do so, while fresh, whole meals are less likely to do so.

Fruits and vegetables are emphasized in an anti-inflammatory diet. Antioxidants may be found in a variety of plant-based meals. However, certain meals may cause the creation of free radicals. Foods that are fried repeatedly in heated cooking oil are an example.

Antioxidants in food are molecules that assist in the removal of free radicals from the body. Somebody activities, such as metabolism, produce free radicals as a natural consequence. External variables like stress and smoking, on the other hand, might raise the quantity of free radicals in the body.

Cell damage may be caused by free radicals. Inflammation is increased as a result of this injury, which may lead to a variety of disorders. The body produces antioxidants that help in the removal of harmful toxins, but dietary antioxidants may also assist.

Anti-inflammatory diets are preferred over foods that stimulate the formation of free radicals in an anti-inflammatory diet.

Omega-3 fatty acids, found in oily fish, may aid in lowering inflammatory protein levels in the body. According to the Arthritis Foundation, fiber can also have this impact.

1.4 Types of Anti-Inflammatory Diet

Anti-inflammatory diets come in a variety of forms. Anti-inflammatory concepts are already included in many popular diets.

For example, Fruits and vegetables, seafood, whole grains, and heart-healthy fats are all part of the Mediterranean and DASH diets.

Although inflammation seems to have an impact on cardiovascular disease, evidence shows that the Mediterranean diet, which emphasizes plant-based foods and healthy oils, may help to minimize inflammation's impact on the cardiovascular system.

1.5 Who can it help?

Many conditions that are worse by chronic inflammation may benefit from an anti-inflammatory diet as a supplemental treatment.

Inflammation involves the following conditions:

- rheumatoid arthritis
- asthma
- psoriasis
- eosinophilic esophagitis
- Hashimoto's thyroiditis
- colitis
- inflammatory bowel disease
- Crohn's disease
- lupus
- metabolic syndrome

Type 2 diabetes, high blood pressure, obesity and cardiovascular disease are all symptoms of metabolic syndrome, which is a collection of illnesses that often occur together.

Inflammation, according to scientists, plays a part in all of these. As a result, an individual with metabolic syndrome may benefit from an anti-inflammatory diet. Consuming an anti-oxidant diet may also assist in reducing the risk of some cancers.

1.6 How Anti-Inflammatory Diet Works?

There isn't a formal diet plan that specifies what to eat, how much to consume, and when to consume it. Instead, the anti-inflammatory diet is eating foods that have been found to reduce inflammation while avoiding items that have been found to increase it.

Consider the anti-inflammatory diet as a way of living rather than a diet, says Brittany Scanniello, a nutritionist in Boulder, Colorado. "Anti-inflammatory diet is a way of eating that works to reduce or reduce low-grade inflammation in our bodies," she explains.

In an ideal world, you'd consume 8 to 9 servings of fruits and vegetables each day, restrict red meat and dairy consumption, favor complex carbs over simple carbs, and avoid processed foods.

Meals high in omega-3 fatty acids, such as anchovies, salmon, halibut, and mussels, are preferable to omega-6 fatty acids, which may be found in maize oil, mayonnaise, vegetables oil, salad dressings, and many processed foods.

According to Scanniello, eating this manner is beneficial for everyone since many of the items that promote inflammation are unhealthy in the first place. "I feel that restricting or eliminating sugar and highly processed meals in favor of unsaturated fats, vegetables, fruits, seeds, nuts and lean meats may help everyone," adds Scanniello.

She believes that an anti-inflammatory diet might be particularly beneficial for those who suffer from chronic inflammation as a consequence of a medical condition. Athletes and others who engage in high-intensity exercise and want to reduce their baseline inflammation may benefit from it, she adds.

1.7 What Research Says About Dietary Inflammation Reduction?

Inflammation has been shown to have harmful consequences in several studies; in fact, chronic inflammatory disorders constitute the leading cause of death worldwide. It's linked to health problems, including diabetes, Alzheimer's, and obesity. According to a June 2019 research published in Nutrients, it has also been linked to increased risk of colorectal cancer, with people who consume pro-inflammatory diets (such as refined carbs and red meat) having a two-fold greater risk of developing the disease. Furthermore, according to a meta-analysis conducted in August 2019 in Clinical Nutrition, a pro-inflammatory diet appears to raise the risk of death by 23% overall.

A number of additional researches have looked at the impact of consuming an anti-inflammatory diet on various health issues. For example, a study published in Frontiers in Nutrition in November 2017 found that eating anti-inflammatory foods may relieve persons with rheumatoid arthritis (RA). When used as a complementary therapy, the authors believe that lowering inflammation in the diet, such as through a vegetarian diet or a vegan, may help delay disease development, minimize joint damage, and perhaps minimize reliance on RA medication. Another small, prospective trial published in 2019 in Integrative Cancer Therapies indicated that persons with familial adenomatous polyposis (colorectal cancer) who followed a low-inflammatory diet had fewer gastrointestinal symptoms and a better overall physical status. An anti-inflammatory diet was associated with a 13 percent decreased risk of cancer mortality in a prospective cohort study of over 68,000 Swedish adults in September 2018, published in Journal of Internal Medicine.

Smokers who followed an anti-inflammatory diet had a 31% reduced chance of dying from any cause, a 36% lower risk of death from cardiovascular disease, as well as a 22% lower chance of death from cancer, according to the researchers. Smoking is a behavior linked to an increased risk of health problems, and sticking to this diet won't guarantee a cure for you if you continue to smoke. Despite this, evidence indicates that it may help to lessen the severity of illness, postpone disease progression, minimize the amount of medicine required, and prevent joint damage.

Anti-inflammatory foods have been proven to assist in the following ways in other studies:

- In sports training, recovery is important.
- Pain connected with aging may be managed in a variety of ways.
- Protection for the heart
- People with multiple sclerosis have a better quality of life.

1.8 Most Anti-Inflammatory Foods to Eat

Inflammation may be bad or good. On the one hand, it helps in the body's defense against infection and injury. Chronic inflammation, on the other hand, may contribute to disease and weight gain. This risk may be increased by stress, inflammatory meals, and a lack of physical exercise. However, research shows that some foods may help to reduce inflammation.

Here are 13 foods that are anti-inflammatory.

1. Berries

Berries are little fruits with a high fiber, vitamin, and mineral content. Although there are many variants, these are a few of the more famous:

- strawberry
- raspberries
- blueberries
- blackberries

Anthocyanins are antioxidants found in berries. These substances have anti-inflammatory effects, which may reduce your disease risk. Natural killer cells are cells produced by your body that help in the normal functioning of your immune system.

Men who consume blueberries every day generated considerably more NK cells than others who did not, according to one research.

Adults with extra weight who consume strawberries had reduced levels of some inflammatory markers linked to heart disease in another research.

2. Fatty Fish

Protein and long-chain omega-3 fatty acids EPA and DHA are abundant in fatty fish. Although all varieties of fish contain some omega-3 fatty acids, these are the best sources:

- salmon
- herring
- sardines
- mackerel
- anchovies

EPA and DHA help to prevent heart disease, metabolic syndrome, diabetes, and kidney disease by reducing inflammation. These fatty acids are metabolized by your body into anti-inflammatory compounds called protectins and resolvins.

People who ate salmon or took EPA and DHA supplements had lower levels of inflammatory marker C-reactive protein, according to studies.

In another research, participants with an unbalanced heartbeat who take EPA and DHA daily had no improvement in inflammatory markers when compared to all those who took a placebo.

3. Broccoli

Broccoli is a nutritious vegetable. And including cauliflower, Brussels sprouts, and kale, it's a cruciferous vegetable. Eating a lot of cruciferous veggies has been linked to a lower risk of heart disease and cancer in studies. This might be due to the antioxidants in them having anti-inflammatory effects. Sulforaphane, an antioxidant found in broccoli, inhibits inflammation by lowering levels of cytokines & NF-kB, which cause inflammation.

4. Avocados

Avocados are also one of the few supposedly superfoods that are really deserving of the name. They're high in potassium, magnesium, fiber, and monounsaturated fats, which are good for your heart.

They also include carotenoids & tocopherols, both of which have been associated with a lower risk of cancer. Avocados also contain a compound that may prevent inflammation in early skin cells.

In one research, persons who ate an avocado slice with their hamburger had low levels of the inflammatory indicators NF-kB and IL-6 than those who ate the hamburger alone.

5. Green Tea

Green tea is among the healthiest teas you can consume, as you've surely heard. It lowers your chances of developing heart disease, Alzheimer's disease, cancer, obesity, and other diseases.

Its antioxidant & anti-inflammatory qualities, particularly a compound called epigallocatechin-3-gallate, are responsible for many of its advantages (EGCG).

EGCG reduces pro-inflammatory cytokine synthesis and fatty acid damage in your cells, which helps to reduce inflammation.

6. Peppers

Bell & chili peppers are high in antioxidants and vitamin C, which have anti-inflammatory effects. The Bell peppers contain antioxidant quercetin, that may help patients with sarcoidosis, an inflammatory disease, lower one indication of oxidative damage. Chili peppers include ferulic acid and sinapic acid, which may help you age better by reducing inflammation.

7. Mushrooms

While there are many species of mushrooms on the planet, just a handful are edible and economically farmed. Truffles, shiitake and portobello mushrooms are among them. Mushrooms are high in selenium, copper, and all of the B vitamins yet are low in calories. They also have anti-inflammatory properties thanks to phenols and other antioxidants.

A type of mushroom known as lion's mane may help to lower low-grade inflammation linked to obesity. Cooking mushrooms, on the other hand, drastically reduced their anti-inflammatory compounds, according to one research. As a result, eating them raw or minimally cooked may be the best option.

8. Grapes

Anthocyanins, which are found in grapes, help to prevent inflammation. They may also reduce the risk of a variety of diseases, like diabetes, heart disease, obesity, Alzheimer's disease, and eye problems. Grapes are also a good source of resveratrol, a compound with a variety of health advantages.

In one research, persons with heart disease who took grape extract on a regular basis noticed their inflammatory gene markers, such as NF-kB, decrease. Furthermore, their adiponectin levels rose. Decreased amounts of this hormone are linked to weight gain and higher cancer risk.

9. Turmeric

Turmeric is an earthy-flavored spice that is commonly used in curries as well as other Dishes. Curcumin, a potent anti-inflammatory substance, has received plenty of attention because of its presence. Turmeric may help with arthritis, diabetes & other inflammatory diseases.

In fact, in persons with metabolic syndrome, taking 1 gram of curcumin daily with piperine from black pepper resulted in a considerable reduction in the inflammatory marker CRP. However, it may be difficult to get enough curcumin from turmeric alone to provide a visible benefit.

In one trial, women who took 2.8 grams of turmeric per day for weight loss showed no change in inflammatory markers. It is much more beneficial to take isolated curcumin supplements. Piperine, which may increase curcumin absorption by two thousand percent, is often coupled with curcumin supplements.

10. Olive Oil Extra Virgin

One of the healthier fats you can consume is extra virgin olive oil. It's high in monounsaturated fats as well as a key component of the Mediterranean diet, which has a long list of health advantages. Extra virgin olive oil has been linked to a lower risk of brain cancer, heart disease and some other major health problems in studies.

CRP and numerous other inflammatory markers fell dramatically in individuals who ingested 1.7 ounces of olive oil daily in one trial on the Mediterranean diet.

Anti-inflammatory medicines like ibuprofen have been likened to the impact of oleocanthal, an antioxidant present in olive oil. It's important to remember that extra virgin olive oil has stronger anti-inflammatory properties than processed olive oils.

11. Cocoa and Dark Chocolate

Dark chocolate is rich, sweet, and satisfying. It's also high in antioxidants, which help to alleviate inflammation. These may lower the risk of disease and help you age more gracefully.

Chocolate's anti-inflammatory properties are due to flavanols, which help maintain the endothelial cells that make up your arteries healthy. In one research, smokers who ate high-flavonol chocolate had significant changes in endothelial function within two hours. To get these anti-inflammatory effects, be sure to purchase dark chocolate that has at least seventy percent cocoa — a higher proportion is even better.

12. Tomatoes

The tomato is a nutrient-dense food. Potassium, Vitamin C and lycopene, an antioxidant with anti-inflammatory qualities, are all abundant in tomatoes. Lycopene may be especially useful in lowering pro-inflammatory compounds linked to a variety of cancers.

According to one research, consuming tomato juice reduced inflammatory markers in people who were overweight but not obese. It's worth noting that cooking tomatoes with olive oil might help you absorb more lycopene. That's because lycopene is carotenoid, a vitamin that absorbs better when consumed with fat.

13. Cherries

Cherries are a delicious fruit. Cherries are sweet and high in anti-inflammatory antioxidants, including anthocyanins and catechins. Although sour cherries have been examined more than other types in terms of their health-promoting characteristics, sweet cherries also give benefits. People who ate 280 grams of cherries per day for a month had lower levels of inflammatory marker CRP, which continued low for another 28 days after they stopped consuming cherries, according to one research.

1.9 Foods That Cause Inflammation

Depending on circumstances, inflammation may be beneficial or harmful. On the one hand, it's your body's natural defense mechanism when you're sick or injured. It can assist your body in fighting sickness and promoting recovery.

Chronic, long-term inflammation, on the other hand, has been associated with an elevated risk of diseases including heart disease, diabetes and obesity. Surprisingly, the things you consume might have a big impact on how much inflammation you have in your body.

Here are six foods that can cause inflammation in the body.

1. High-fructose corn syrup and sugar

The two primary kinds of added sugar in the Western diet are table sugar & high fructose corn syrup (HFCS). High fructose corn syrup is around 45 percent glucose and 55 percent fructose, while sugar is 50 percent glucose and 50 percent fructose. Increased inflammation, which may lead to illness, is one of the reasons why additional sugars are hazardous. Mice on high-sugar diets developed breast cancer that migrated to their lungs, in part owing to the inflammatory reaction to sugar.

The anti-inflammatory benefits of omega-3 fatty acids were reduced in mice given a high-sugar diet in another research. Furthermore, in a randomized clinical experiment in which participants drank regular diet soda, soda, milk or water, only those who drank normal soda had higher uric acid levels, which causes inflammation and insulin resistance.

Sugar also is harmful since it contains an excessive quantity of fructose. While moderate quantities of fructose in vegetables and fruits are OK, ingesting high quantities of fructose from added sugars is indeed not. Obesity, diabetes, insulin resistance, cancer, fatty liver disease and chronic kidney disease have all been related to eating much fructose.

Fructose also induces inflammation in the endothelial cells that make up line your blood arteries, which is a risk factor for heart disease, according to studies. In mice and humans, high fructose consumption has been demonstrated to enhance many inflammatory markers. Chocolate, candy, cakes, soft drinks, cookies, sweet pastries, doughnuts and some cereals are all rich in added sugar.

2. Artificial Trans Fat

Artificial trans fats are among the unhealthiest fats you may consume. They are made by adding hydrogen to liquid unsaturated fats to give them the consistency of solid fat. Trans fats are often indicated as partly hydrogenated oils on ingredient labels. Trans fats are found in most margarine and are often used to improve the shelf life of processed foods.

Artificial trans fats, unlike naturally produced trans fats present in dairy and meat, have been demonstrated to promote inflammation and raise disease risk. Trans fats may affect the function of endothelial cells that line your arteries, which is a major risk factor for the heart, in addition to reducing HDL (good) cholesterol.

Artificial trans-fat consumption has been related to elevated levels of inflammatory indicators, including C-reactive protein (CRP). CRP levels were 78 percent higher in one research among women who reported the greatest trans-fat consumption. Hydrogenated soybean oil elevated inflammation substantially more than palm and sunflower oils in a randomized controlled experiment including older ladies with excess weight.

Inflammatory indicators increased in both healthy men and individuals with high cholesterol levels in response to trans fats, according to studies.

French fries and other fried fast food, certain microwave popcorn variations, some vegetable shortenings and margarines, packaged cakes and cookies, certain pastries, and other processed goods with partly hydrogenated vegetable oil on the label are high in trans fats.

3. Seeds and Vegetable Oils

Vegetable oil consumption in United States climbed by 130 percent throughout the twentieth century. Because of their high omega-6 fatty acid concentration, some experts think that some vegetable oils, like soybean oil, increase inflammation. Although certain omega-6 fats are required in the diet, the normal Western diet gives significantly more than is required. To increase your ratio, omega-6 to omega-3 and gain the anti-inflammatory effects of omega-3s, health authorities suggest consuming more omega-3-rich foods, like fatty fish.

In one research, rats given a diet with a 20:1 omega-6 to omega-3 ratio showed significantly greater levels of inflammatory markers than rats on a 1:1 or 5:1 diet.

However, there is presently little evidence that high consumption of omega-6 fatty acids causes inflammation in people. Linoleic acid, the most prevalent dietary omega-6 acid, has been shown in controlled experiments to have no effect on inflammatory markers. Before any judgments can be made, further investigation is required.

Cooking oils made from vegetables and seeds are a common element in processed meals.

4. Refined carbohydrates

Carbohydrates also have a bad reputation. The fact is that not all carbohydrates are bad for you. For millennia, ancient people ate grasses, roots, and fruits, which were rich in fiber and unprocessed carbohydrates. Consumption of refined carbohydrates, on the other hand, may lead to inflammation.

The majority of the fiber has been eliminated from refined carbohydrates. Fiber keeps you fuller for longer, helps blood sugar regulation, and feeds your intestinal microbes. The processed carbohydrate in today's diet, according to researchers, may promote the development of inflammatory gut bacteria, raising your risk of obesity as well as inflammatory bowel disease.

The glycemic index (GI) of refined carbohydrates is greater than that of unprocessed carbohydrates. Meals with a high GI spike blood sugar levels faster than foods with a low GI.

In one research, older persons who ate the most high-GI meals had a 2.9-fold increased risk of dying from an inflammatory condition like (COPD) chronic obstructive pulmonary disease. Young, healthy males who ate 50 grams of refined carbohydrates in the form of white bread had high blood sugar levels and increased levels of a specific inflammatory marker in controlled research.

Candy, pasta, pastries, bread, certain cereals, cakes, cookies, sugary soft drinks, and any processed meals with added sugar or wheat include refined carbs.

5. Drinking too much Alcohol

Alcohol use in moderation has been found to have certain health advantages. Higher doses, on the other hand, might cause serious difficulties.

In one research, participants who drank Alcohol had higher levels of inflammatory marker CRP. Their CRP levels rose in direct proportion to the amount of Alcohol they ingested.

People who consume large amounts of Alcohol may have issues with bacterial toxins migrating out of the colon and into the body. This disorder, often known as "leaky gut," may cause extensive inflammation and organ damage.

To prevent alcohol-related health concerns, males should have no more than two standard drinks each day and women should have no more than one.

6. Processed Meat

Processed meat consumption has been linked to a higher risk of diabetes, heart disease and colon & stomach cancer. Bacon, sausage, ham, smoked meat and beef jerky are all examples of processed meat.

More new glycation end products (AGEs) are found in processed meat than in most other meats. AGEs are generated when meats and other foods are cooked at high temperatures. They have a history of causing inflammation.

The relationship between processed meat intake and colon cancer is the sharpest of all the disorders associated with it. Although several variables play a role in colon cancer, one mechanism is thought to be the inflammatory response of colon cells to processed meat.

Inflammation may be triggered by a variety of factors, some of which are difficult to avoid, such as injury, pollution or sickness.

You do, however, have a lot more influence over things like your food.

Reduce inflammation by limiting your intake of items that cause it and consuming anti-inflammatory nutrients to remain as healthy as possible.

1.10 Diet Tips to Help You Fight Inflammation

Choosing entire meals like fruits, vegetables & whole grains over processed meals has several health advantages. One of the most important advantages of these nutrient-dense meals is their ability to decrease inflammation in the body.

"Exercise can create short-term inflammation or acute, that is normal," explains Kate Patton, RD, MEd, CSSD, LD, a sports health dietitian. "A healthy diet may help keep inflammation under control."

The risk of chronic inflammation as a consequence of poor diet, stress, and/or incorrect or overtraining in people who exercise regularly is particularly alarming. The above combination puts you at a greater risk of being injured or sick. Reduced inflammation in the body may help you exercise more regularly, heal quicker from injuries, operate at your best, and, in the end, avoid chronic illness.

Because they are your supplies of energy (carbs), the basic building block of cells (protein), and the way to absorb vitamins (fat), foods that treat inflammation have a mixture of carbohydrates, protein, and fat (fat). Muscle contraction, tissue repair, blood flow and healing are all helped by vitamins and minerals.

Dietary Recommendations for Food

Patton offers nine dietary guidelines for reducing inflammation:

- Whole-grain carbohydrates, pure whole fruits and veggies are the best options. These are higher in nutritional density and include a wide range of minerals and vitamins that are essential for maintaining and improving health.
- To get the most nutritious bang for your money, rotate among a range of colorful fruits, veggies, and grains from week to week.
- Refined starches (white variants) and added sugars should be avoided (brown or white sugar, energy drinks, soda). Inflammatory symptoms, including weight gain and increased blood glucose and cholesterol levels, are promoted by these less nutrient-dense diets.
- Skinless chicken, fish, eggs, lentils, and fat-free Greek yogurt are also good choices. These are high-quality protein sources with added calcium, vitamin D, probiotics, and unsaturated fat.
- Processed meats like salami, bologna and hot dogs, as well as high-fat red meats like prime rib, bacon, and sausage, should be avoided. These are high in saturated fat, which may cause inflammation if ingested in excess.
- Omega-3 and Monounsaturated fats are recommended because they are thought to reduce inflammation. Olive oil, avocados, and almonds all contain monounsaturated fats. Consumption of these fats has been linked to a lower risk of cancer and heart disease, both of which are linked to inflammation.
- Tuna and wild salmon, walnuts, and ground flaxseed all contain omega-3 fatty acids. Omega-3 is an important fatty acid that our systems cannot produce and must be obtained via food or supplementation.
- Saturated fat should be avoided. Whole milk, cheese, butter, high-fat red meat, and chicken skin all fall under this category. Because our bodies only need a tiny quantity, every day over consumption will increase the inflammatory response.
- Trans fat should be avoided if possible. While trans fats have been prohibited in most foods by the FDA, they may still be found in products like flavored coffee creamers and microwave popcorn. As a result, make sure to read labels carefully. There is no such thing as a safe level of trans fat. It not only lowers good cholesterol while raising bad cholesterol (a pro-inflammatory factor), but it also reuses and recycles it.

Find Vitamins in foods you consume

Here are some suggestions that are most effective for people who exercise frequently:

- **Vitamin A:** is found in sweet potatoes, spinach, carrots, and tomatoes, among other foods.
- **Vitamin C:** is present in fruits and vegetables such as citrus, cantaloupe, and green & red peppers.
- **Vitamin D:** Oily fish, fortified meals, and dairy products are all good sources of vitamin D.
- **Calcium:** Cheese, low-fat milk, kale, broccoli, fortified orange juice, low-fat Greek yogurt, and fortified non-dairy milk are all good sources of calcium.
- **Copper:** To obtain your copper, eat pumpkin, sesame, shitake mushrooms, sunflower seeds and pumpkin, and cashews. Copper is also beneficial during the first several weeks after an injury (a sufficient quantity can be found in a normal multivitamin).
- **Zinc:** Eat crabmeat, chicken, lean beef, cashews, and fortified cereals to increase your zinc intake.
- **Turmeric:** Turmeric is a spice that may be found in curry powder. Curcumin is an anti-inflammatory, antioxidant chemical found in turmeric, which provides mustard and curries their yellow color. Probably add turmeric to your spice cabinet, or take 400 milligrams of turmeric daily in pill form for a more aggressive approach.
- **Garlic:** It may help maintain arteries flexible and clean, enabling oxygen-rich blood to reach working muscles by reducing the production of 2 inflammatory enzymes. Cooking with 2 to 4 garlic cloves each day will enhance taste and help to reduce inflammation.
- **Bromelain:** Bromelain is a pineapple-derived enzyme. After your exercise, drink one glass of pineapple juice or include it in your recovery smoothie for lots of immune-boosting vitamin C & inflammation-fighting effects.

"It's important to think about how you nourish your body," she advises. "A healthy diet and vitamins may help keep inflammation under control."

1.11 Anti-Inflammatory Diet Plan

The instance menu below is not one-size-fits-all, but it does provide some inventive ways to include anti-inflammatory items into your meals. You may have nutritional needs this meal plan does not meet if you are managing a disease like diabetes. Before making any big changes to your food habits, consult your healthcare team.

A 7-Day Anti-Inflammatory Diet Sample Menu for Beginners

Day 1

- **Breakfast** Steel-cut oats with almonds & blueberries for breakfast, along with a cup of coffee.
- **Lunch** Salad of chopped kale, chickpeas, beets & pomegranate seeds with olive oil and also lemon juice vinaigrette for lunch.
- **Dinner** Pizza with anchovies, fish, and tomatoes on a cauliflower crust.
- **Snack** Snack time a small handful of unsalted nuts & raisins in a homemade trail mix

Day 2

- **Breakfast** Steel-cut oats with sliced strawberries and walnuts for breakfast; a cup of coffee.
- **Lunch** Salmon sashimi with broccoli and brown rice, topped with ginger.
- **Dinner** Whitefish, barley, kale in a ginger curry.
-
- **Snack** Mango slices

Day 3

- **Breakfast** A cup of green tea and a quinoa dish with blueberries, sliced banana, and a drizzle of almond butter.
- **Lunch** Salad of arugula with grilled peaches, albacore tuna and walnuts for lunch.
- **Dinner** Spinach salad with grilled fish and brown rice for dinner.
- **Snack** Frozen grapes.

Day 4

- **Breakfast** Frittata with kale and mushrooms, half a grapefruit also a cup of coffee.
- **Lunch** Brown rice, sautéed bok choy and chickpeas in a grain bowl for lunch.
- **Dinner** Veggie burger on a whole-wheat bun with roasted Brussels sprouts on the side
- **Snack** Small unsalted mixed nuts as a snack.

Day 5

- **Breakfast** A cup of green tea, chia seed pudding, and apple with almond butter.
- **Lunch** Salad with spinach, tuna, and shredded carrots.
- **Dinner** Stuffed red peppers with ground turkey, chickpeas and quinoa.
- **Snack** Snack time Unsalted almonds, little handful.

Day 6

- **Breakfast** A cup of coffee and soy yogurt with fresh blueberries
- **Lunch** Sardines, black beans, tomatoes, avocado and sautéed spinach in a quinoa bowl for lunch.
- **Dinner** Spinach salad and salmon with lentils for dinner.
- **Snack** A modest handful of unsalted mixed nuts with a piece of dark chocolate.

Day 7

- **Breakfast** A cup of coffee with a peanut butter & banana sandwich.
- **Lunch** Halved cherry tomatoes and Smashed avocado over whole-grain bread with cottage cheese on the side.
- **Dinner** Seitan stir-fried in olive oil with mushrooms, bell peppers and broccoli.
- **Snack** Cherries.

Chapter 2: Breakfast Recipes

2.1 Smoothie with cherries and mocha

Ready in 10 min
Servings: 2
Difficulty: Easy
Ingredients

- 2 tbsp of cocoa powder
- 2 tbsp almond butter
- 2 cups of ice cubes
- 1 teaspoon coffee powder
- 1 teaspoon of vanilla
- 1 cup frozen dark sweet cherries
- 1 cup chocolate almond milk
- 5.3 to 6-ounce carton vanilla fat-free yogurt
- ½ banana
- 1 tbsp of Dark chocolate

Instructions

1) Mix almond milk, yogurt, cherries, banana, cocoa powder, almond milk, proper coffee powder, and vanilla in a blender and mix until smooth. Blend until smooth, covered. Cover and mix until smooth, adding ice cubes as needed. Pour into glasses and garnish with chocolate-covered espresso beans, chocolate shavings, and more banana slices, if desired.

2.2 Omelet with avocado and kale

Ready in 10 min **Servings:** 1
Difficulty: Easy

Ingredients

- 1 teaspoon sunflower seeds
- 2 teaspoons of extra-virgin olive oil
- 1 tbsp lemon juice
- Pinch of salt
- ¼ avocado, sliced
- 2 eggs
- 1 teaspoon low-fat milk
- Pinch of crushed red pepper
- salt
- 1 tbsp chopped cilantro
- 1 cup chopped kale

Instructions

1) In a small bowl, whisk together the eggs, milk, and salt. In a small fry pan, heat 1 teaspoon oil over medium heat. Cook for 2 minutes, just until the base is set, but the middle is still a little runny. Cook for another 30 seconds on the other side or until the omelet is set. Place on a platter to cool.

2) Toss the kale with leftover 1 teaspoon oil, lemon juice, cilantro, sunflower seeds, smashed red pepper, and a sprinkle of salt in a large mixing bowl. Avocado and kale salad goes on top of the omelet.

2.3 Breakfast Salad with Baby Kale, Quinoa, and Strawberries

Ready in 15 min **Servings:** 1 **Difficulty** Easy
Ingredients

- 1 tbsp olive oil
- 2 teaspoons vinegar
- 3 cups packed baby kale
- ½ cup cooked quinoa
- Pinch of pepper
- ½ cup sliced strawberries
- 1 tbsp pepitas
- 1 teaspoon garlic
- Pinch of salt

Instructions

1) To make a paste, mash the garlic & salt, including the side of even a chef's knife or a fork. In a medium mixing bowl, combine the oil, garlic paste, vinegar, and pepper. Stir in the kale and toss to coat. Serve with quinoa, strawberries, and pepitas on the side.

2.4 Lemony Labneh with Pistachios

Ready in 12 hrs.
Servings: 8
Difficulty: Easy
Ingredients

- 4 cups of low-fat plain yogurt
- 1 tbsp olive oil or agrumato lemon oil
- 1 tbsp fresh parsley, chopped
- 1 teaspoon of lemon zest
- ¼ teaspoon of salt
- ¼ cup pistachios
- ¼ teaspoon of ground sumac

Instructions

1) Multiple levels of cheesecloth should be used to line a 7-inch and larger fine-mesh sieve. Place over a dish deep enough to allow at least four inches between the sieve's bottom and the bowl's bottom. In a larger bowl, whisk together the yogurt and salt; pour into the cheesecloth.
2) Refrigerate for 12 to 24 hours, or until the yogurt is quite thick, as well as at least a single cup of water has dripped into the bowl. (Remove the liquid.)
3) Sprinkle with lemon zest, oil, pistachios, parsley and sumac to serve.

2.5 Toast with Mascarpone and Berries

Ready in 5 min **Servings:** 1
Difficulty: Easy

Ingredients

- 1 slice toasted whole-grain bread
- 1 teaspoon of mint leaves
- ¼ cup of berries, such as blueberries, raspberries
- 2 tbsp of cheese

Instructions

1) Mascarpone, berries, and mint go on top of the bread.

2.6 Granola Bars with Almond Joy

Ready in 1 hr. 30 min
Servings: 24
Difficulty: Easy
Ingredients

- ¼ teaspoon of salt
- ⅔ cup of brown rice syrup
- ½ cup almond butter
- 1 teaspoon of coconut extract
- 3 cups oats
- 1 cup brown rice cereal, crispy
- 1 cup of chocolate chips
- 1 cup shredded coconut, toasted

Instructions

1) Heat the oven to 325 ° F.
2) Using parchment paper, line a 9-by-13-inch baking sheet, with excess parchment falling over two edges. Spray the parchment lightly with cooking spray.
3) In a large mixing bowl, combine the chocolate chips, cereal, shredded coconut, oats and salt.
4) In a microwave-safe bowl, mix rice syrup, coconut essence and almond butter, 30 seconds in the microwave. Stir in the wet ingredients until everything is well mixed. Move to the prepared baking dish and use the edge of a spatula to firmly press the dough into the pan.

5) For creamier texture bars, bake for 20 to 25 minutes, or until just beginning to brown around the edges and still moist in the center. Bake for 35 minutes, or until lightly browned around the edges and somewhat hard in the center, for crunchier bars.

6) Allow cooling throughout the pan for 10 minutes before lifting out onto a cutting board with the aid of the parchment paper. Cut into 24 pieces, then set aside for another 30 minutes to cool fully without splitting the bars. Separate the mixture into bars after it has cooled.

2.7 Smoothie with Peanut Butter and Jelly

Ready in 5 min
Servings: 1
Difficulty: Easy
Ingredients

- 1 cup f banana slices
- ½ cup frozen strawberries
- 1 tbsp peanut butter
- 1 cup of spinach
- 2 teaspoons maple syrup
- ½ cup of low-fat milk
- ⅓ cup plain yogurt

Instructions

1) In a blender, combine the yogurt & milk, then add the banana, spinach, strawberries, peanut butter, and sweetener; mix until smooth.

2.8 Baked Oatmeal with Banana, Raisins, and Walnuts

Ready in 1 hr. 5 min
Servings: 6
Difficulty: Easy

Ingredients

- 1 teaspoon of vanilla extract
- 1 banana, sliced
- ⅓ cup of raisins
- 1 teaspoon of baking powder
- ½ teaspoon of salt
- ¼ teaspoon of ground allspice
- 2 cups milk
- ¾ cup yogurt
- 2 tbsp canola oil
- ¼ cup brown sugar
- 2 cups oats
- ⅓ cup chopped walnuts
- 1 ½ teaspoons cinnamon

Instructions

1) Preheat the oven to 375 Fahrenheit. Using cooking spray, prepare an 8-inch-square baking dish.

2) In a large mixing basin, combine the walnuts, oats, cinnamon, salt, baking powder, and allspice. In a medium mixing bowl, combine the milk, yogurt, oil, brown sugar, and vanilla. Stir the milk mixture into the dry ingredients until everything is well combined. Combine the bananas and raisins in a mixing bowl. Slowly pour into the baking dish that has been prepared.

3) Bake for 45 to 50 minutes, or until brown on top & firm to the touch.

2.9 Pancakes with Avocado

Ready in 35 min
Servings: 4
Difficulty: Easy
Ingredients

- 1 cup almond milk
- ⅓ cup ripe avocado
- 2 tbsp sugar
- 1 teaspoon of lemon zest
- 2 tbsp flaxseed meal

- 5 tbsp water
- 1 teaspoon of vanilla extract
- ¼ teaspoon of salt
- 1 teaspoon of baking powder
- 1 teaspoon of canola oil
- ¼ cup of Blueberries
- ¼ teaspoon spirulina powder
- 1 ⅓ cups gluten-free flour

Instructions

1) In a small dish, combine a flaxseed meal and water. Stir in the water well. Allow for a 5-minute rest period.
2) In a blender, purée the almond milk, lemon zest, sugar, avocado, vanilla, salt, and spirulina until smooth, approximately 1 minute. Place in a large mixing basin. Combine the flaxseed and water in a mixing bowl.
3) In a medium mixing bowl, whisk together the flour and baking powder; incorporate into avocado mixture.
4) Preheat a medium-sized nonstick pan or griddle. Spread a thin coating of oil in the pan using a paper towel. For each pancake, use 1/4 cup batter and carefully spread in 3 1/2-inch rounds. Cook the pancakes for 4 to 5 minutes on each side until it's browned and cooked through. Rep with the rest of the batter. If desired, top with blueberries.

2.10 Burrata and Avocado Toast

Ready in 5 min
Servings: 1
Difficulty: Easy
Ingredients

- ⅛ teaspoon of ground pepper
- 1 ounce of Burrata
- 1 teaspoon of lemon juice
- 1 teaspoon basil, finely sliced
- 1 teaspoon chives, minced
- Aleppo pepper

- 1 slice of whole-grain toast
- ½ large thinly sliced ripe avocado
- ⅛ teaspoon of salt

Instructions

1) Avocado should be spread on the bread. Season with salt and pepper, then sprinkle with lemon juice. Burrata chives, basil, and Aleppo pepper are served on top.

2.11 Smoothie with strawberries, blueberries, and bananas

Ready in 5 min
Servings: 1
Difficulty: Easy
Ingredients

- ½ cup of strawberries
- ¾ cup of cashew milk
- 1 tbsp of butter
- ½ cup of blueberries
- 1 small ripe banana(optional)
- 1 tbsp of hulled hemp seeds

Instructions

1) In a blender, combine the blueberries, strawberries, banana, cashew butter, cashew milk, and hemp seeds. Blend until smooth, adding additional cashew milk if necessary to get the appropriate consistency. Serve right away.

2.12 Overnight Oatmeal with Dates and Pine Nuts

Ready in 8 hrs. **Servings:** 1 **Difficulty:** Easy

Ingredients

- Pinch of salt
- 2 tbsp dates, chopped

- 1 tbsp pine nuts, toasted
- ½ cup rolled oats
- ½ cup of water
- ¼ teaspoon of cinnamon
- 1 teaspoon of honey

Instructions

1) Stir together the oats, water, & salt inside a jar or basin. Refrigerate overnight, covered.
2) Heat the oats in the morning are preferred, or eat them cold. Dates, pine nuts, honey, and cinnamon are sprinkled over the top.

2.13 Pancakes with Orange Whole-Wheat Flour

Ready in 30 min
Servings: 6
Difficulty: Easy
Ingredients

- 3 oranges
- 1 cup buttermilk
- ½ teaspoon of baking soda
- 1 teaspoon of vanilla extract
- 2 tbsp brown sugar
- 2 tbsp of canola oil
- 1 ½ cups whole-wheat flour
- 3 tbsp of flax meal
- 2 eggs
- 1 teaspoon baking powder
- ¼ teaspoon of ground ginger
- ⅛ teaspoon salt

Instructions

1) In a large mixing bowl, combine baking powder, flour, flax meal, baking soda, ginger, and salt.
2) To acquire 1 tbsp of zest, zest 1 orange. 1/4 cup juice may be obtained by juicing it. The two remaining oranges should be cut into halves. Set aside the parts after cutting them into thirds.

3) In a medium mixing basin, whisk together vanilla, orange juice, brown sugar, eggs, buttermilk, oil, and zest.
4) Combine the wet and dry ingredients in a mixing bowl and whisk until just blended. Do not over mix the ingredients. At the same time, you warm the pan, set aside the batter for 5 minutes.
5) Spray a large nonstick skillet or griddle lightly with cooking spray & heat over medium-high heat. 1/3 cup batter each pancake is dropped into the heated pan. Cook the pancakes for 4 minutes till they start to bubble, then flip & cook for another 3 minutes until gently browned on the other side.
6) Rep with the rest of the batter. Warm the pancakes in a 200°F oven until you're ready to eat them. Serve with the orange segments that were set aside.

2.14 Scrambled Eggs with Smoked Trout and Spinach

Ready in 15 min
Servings: 2
Difficulty: Easy
Ingredients
- 4 eggs
- ¼ teaspoon ground pepper
- Salt
- 2 tbsp shallot, finely chopped
- 2 teaspoons seed oil
- ½ cup boned & flaked smoked trout
- 2 tbsp milk
- 1 cup spinach, chopped

Instructions

1) In a medium mixing bowl, whisk together the eggs, milk, pepper, and salt until light yellow all over.
2) In a big nonstick skillet, heat the oil over medium heat. Cook, occasionally stirring, until the shallot begins to brown, about 1 to 2 minutes. Reduce the heat to medium-low and add the egg mixture. Cook, occasionally stirring, until the edges begin to set, approximately 30 seconds. Trout should be strewn over the eggs. Gently press and fold the eggs with a rubber spatula until frothy & barely set, 2 to 4 minutes. Add the spinach and mix well. Remove from the heat, cover, set aside for 2 minutes, or until spinach is barely wilted.

2.15 Breakfast with Greek Yogurt

Ready in 10 min
Servings: 1
Difficulty: Easy
Ingredients
- ¾ cup yogurt
- ¾ cup of vegetable juice
- 1 cup carrots
- ¾ cup of blueberries
- 2 slices toasted whole-grain bread

Instructions

1) On a platter or in separate containers, arrange carrots, Greek yogurt, and bread. Serve with vegetable juice that is low in salt.
2) To round up this well-balanced dinner, serve with blueberries.

2.16 Oranges with Cinnamon

Ready in 10 min
Servings: 4
Difficulty: Easy

Ingredients
- 2 tbsp lemon juice
- 1 tbsp sugar
- 4 navel oranges
- 2 tbsp orange juice
- ¼ teaspoon cinnamon

Instructions

1) Remove the rind & white pith from the oranges using a sharp knife. Cut each into five or six slices and place them on four plates. Combine the orange and lemon juices, sugar, and cinnamon in a mixing bowl. Spread the orange slices on top.

2.17 Blood Oranges with Yogurt and Cardamom Brulle

Ready in 15 min
Servings: 4
Difficulty: Easy
Ingredients
- 1 teaspoon g cardamom
- 1 cup yogurt
- 4 oranges
- 8 teaspoons brown sugar

Instructions

1) Preheat the broiler and place the rack in the top third of the oven (if you have a culinary blowtorch, you can use it instead). Using foil, line a baking pan.
2) Halve the oranges crosswise. Cut the base of each half with a sharp blade or paring knife, so it rests without rolling. Remove any seeds by cutting over each segment. Make a cross in the middle of the fruit and run the knife from around the edge without cutting into the white pith. Place them cut-side up orange halves on the preheated pan.

3) In a small bowl, mix brown sugar and cardamom. 1 teaspoon over top of each half of an orange 3 to 5 minutes under the broiler, until the top is caramelized. Serve with a side of yogurt.

2.18 Energy Bites from Carrot Cake

Ready in 15 min
Servings: 22
Difficulty: Easy
Ingredients
- ¾ teaspoon cinnamon
- ¼ teaspoon g turmeric
- ¼ teaspoon of salt
- Pinch of pepper
- ½ teaspoon ginger
- 1 teaspoon vanilla extract
- 1 cup dates
- ½ cup of rolled oats
- ¼ cup of chia seeds
- 2 finely chopped carrots
- ¼ cup chopped pecans

Instructions

1) In a food processor, mix dates, oats, pecans, & chia seeds; pulse until thoroughly blended and diced.
2) Process carrots, vanilla, cardamom, ginger, turmeric, salt, & pepper in a food processor until thoroughly diced and a paste form.
3) Using only a little 1 tbsp. of the ingredients, roll into balls.

2.19 Apple Butter with Chai in the Slow Cooker

Ready in 7 hrs. 45 min
Servings: 28
Difficulty: Easy
Ingredients
- 2 teaspoons cardamom
- 2 teaspoons cinnamon
- 2 teaspoons turmeric
- ½ teaspoon of salt
- 2 teaspoons coriander
- 5 pounds apples
- ⅔ cup brown sugar
- 1 tbsp of vanilla extract

Instructions

1) In a 6-quart or larger slow cooker, mix apple, turmeric, brown sugar, cardamom, vanilla, cinnamon, coriander, and salt. Cover and cook on high for 5 hours, stirring once or twice. Set the cover ajar and simmer, stirring regularly, for another 2 hours, until the apples become practically broken down. Puree in a mixing bowl until smooth, if desired.

2.20 Smoothie with Anti-Inflammatory Cherry and Spinach

Ready in 5 min
Servings: 1
Difficulty: Easy
Ingredients
- 1 cup plain kefir
- 1 cup cherries
- ½ cup spinach leaves
- ¼ cup ripe avocado
- 1 tbsp salted almond butter
- 1 piece ginger
- 1 teaspoon chia seeds, plus more for garnish

Instructions

1) In a blender, combine the kefir and the water. Puree the spinach, cherries, avocado, ginger, almond butter and chia seeds in a high-powered blender until smooth. Put into a glass and, if preferred, top with extra chia seeds.

2.21 Spinach, Tomato, and Feta Waffle

Ready in 10 min
Servings: 1
Difficulty: Easy
Ingredients

- 1 whole-grain waffle
- 3 quartered cherry tomatoes
- 1 tbsp feta cheese
- 1/4 cup spinach

Instructions

1) Waffles should be toasted according to the package guidelines. Top with spinach, tomatoes, and feta cheese on a platter. Serve right away.

2.22 Overnight Oats with Cherry and Walnuts

Ready in 8 hrs.
Servings: 1
Difficulty: Easy
Ingredients

- 1 tbsp dried cherries, chopped
- 1 tbsp chopped walnuts, toasted
- 2 teaspoons of raw sugar
- ½ teaspoon of lemon zest
- ½ cup of rolled oats
- ½ cup of water
- Pinch of salt
- 2 tbsp cream cheese

Instructions

1) Stir together the oats, water, & salt inside a jar or basin. Refrigerate overnight, covered.
2) Heat the oats in the morning if preferred, or eat them cold. Whipped cream, cherries, walnuts, sugar, and lemon zest go on top.

2.23 Smoothie with berries and kefir

Ready in 5 min
Servings: 1
Difficulty: Easy
Ingredients

- ½ banana
- 2 teaspoons of almond butter
- 1 ½ cups of mixed berries
- 1 cup of plain kefir
- ½ teaspoon of vanilla extract

Instructions

1) In a blender, combine the berries, banana, kefir, almond butter, and vanilla. Blend until completely smooth.

2.24 Quinoa Cakes from Southwest

Ready in 1 hr.
Servings: 6
Difficulty: Easy
Ingredients

- 14-ounce can of fire-roasted diced tomatoes
- 1 clove of garlic
- 1 chipotle pepper in adobo sauce
- ¼ cup cilantro, chopped
- 1 chopped avocado
- ¾ cup cottage cheese
- ¼ cup scallions, sliced
- 2 tbsp flour
- 1 teaspoon of baking powder
- 1/4 teaspoon salt
- 1 cup shredded pepper
- 2 cups of water
- 1 cup red quinoa
- 4 lightly beaten eggs
- 1 cup rinsed canned black beans

Instructions

1) Preheat the oven to 375 Fahrenheit. Using cooking spray, spray a 12-cup nonstick baking tray.

2) In a medium saucepan, bring to a boil. Add the quinoa and mix well. Reduce to low heat, cover, and cook for 15 minutes, just until the grains become soft and expose their spiraling germ. Allow it cool for 10 minutes in a large mixing basin.

3) Toss the quinoa with the eggs, flour, beans, scallions, cottage cheese, baking powder, and 1/4 teaspoon salt until completely blended. 1/4 cup each) of the mixture should be divided among the muffin cups. 1 tablespoon cheese on top of each quinoa cake.

4) Step 4 Bake the cakes for approximately 20 minutes, or until puffed and golden brown on top. Allow cooling for 5 minutes in the pan. With a paring knife, gently loosen and remove.

5) In a blender, purée the tomatoes, garlic, chipotle pepper, and a touch of salt until smooth. Stir in the cilantro in a small mixing bowl.

6) Toss the cakes with both the salsa & avocado before serving.

2.25 Sandwich with egg and salmon

Ready in 15 min
Servings: 1
Difficulty: Easy
Ingredients
- 1/2 teaspoon chopped capers
- 1 ounce of smoked salmon
- 1 whole-wheat toasted English muffin
- ½ teaspoon of virgin olive oil
- 1 slice of tomato
- 1 tbsp red onion, chopped
- 2 beaten egg whites
- Pinch salt

Instructions
1) In a medium nonstick skillet, heat the oil over medium heat. Cook, occasionally stirring, until the onion starts to soften, approximately 1 minute. Add the egg whites, salt, & capers to cook, frequently stirring, for approximately 30 seconds or until the whites are set.

2) Place the smoked salmon, egg whites, and tomato on an English muffin to construct the sandwich.

2.26 Recipe for maple-baked rice porridge with fruit

Ready in 35 min
Servings: 2
Difficulty: Easy
Ingredients
- ½ cup of brown rice
- Pinch of salt
- ½ teaspoon of vanilla extract
- 2 tbsp maple syrup
- Sliced fruit, such as plums, pears, berries, or cherries
- Pinch of cinnamon

Instructions
1) Preheat oven to 400 °F.

2) In a medium-high-heat saucepan, combine the rice & 1 cup of water. Bring to a boil, and then mix in the vanilla extract & cinnamon. Turn down the heat to moderate and cover. Simmer for 10-15 minutes (or according to package instructions if using a rice type that takes longer to prepare) or until soft.

3) Stir the rice and divide it into two heat-safe dishes. Add a spoonful of maple syrup & your favorite sliced fruit to each bowl. If desired, season with salt.

4) Bake for 15 minutes or until maple syrup begins to bubble and the fruit begins to caramelize. Serve right away.

2.27 Herb-Baked Eggs in 5 Minutes

Ready in 5 min
Servings: 1
Difficulty: Easy
Ingredients
- 1 teaspoon butter, melted
- The sprinkling of dried oregano, garlic powder, dried thyme, dried parsley, & dried dill
- 2 eggs
- 1 tbsp milk

Instructions
1) Preheat the oven to "Broil" on low.
2) Using the butter and milk, cover the base of a medium baking dish.
3) Crack the eggs over the butter and milk mixture. Garlic and dry herbs are sprinkled over the top.
4) Cook for 5minutes, just until the eggs become fully cooked.

2.28 Parfait with Coffee & Mint Yogurt

Ready in 20 min
Servings: 1
Difficulty: Easy
Ingredients
- 3-4 peppermint Stevia drops
- ¼ cup pecans, chopped
- 2 teaspoons coffee
- ½ cup yogurt
- coffee granules & fresh mint

Instructions
1) In a small mixing dish, combine the yogurt, coffee, & stevia (if using).
2) In a tiny glass, alternate layers of yogurt and pecans until you reach the top.
3) Add coffee granules & fresh mint on the top.

2.29 Cinnamon Granola with a Crunchy

Ready in 30 min
Servings: 1
Difficulty: Easy
Ingredients
- 2 cups rolled oats
- ¼ cup shredded coconut
- ¼ cup walnuts, chopped
- ¼ teaspoon of cloves
- 2 tbsp pumpkin seeds
- ½ teaspoon of cinnamon
- ¼ teaspoon nutmeg
- ¼ cup of honey
- 4 tbsp butter, melted
- ¼ cup raisins
- ¼ cup apricots, chopped
- ¼ cup cranberries

Instructions
1) Heat oven to 350°F. Prepare a baking sheet.
2) Mix the oats, pumpkin seeds, coconuts, walnuts, and spices in a big mixing basin and set aside.
3) In a separate dish, mix the honey & melted butter and pour over the oat mixture. Stir everything together well.
4) Pour the oat mixture onto the baking sheet and spread it out evenly. Bake for about 25 minutes, or until golden brown. Remove from the oven and set aside to cool.
5) Once the granola has cooled, break it up and toss it inside the dried fruit. Keep the container sealed.

2.30 Anti-Inflammatory Smoothie with Energizing Pineapple

Ready in 10 min
Servings: 1
Difficulty: Easy
Ingredients

- 2/3 cup of cucumber
- ½ cup mango chunks
- ½ of the banana
- 1/2" fresh ginger
- ¼ teaspoon turmeric
- 3 mint leaves, chopped
- 1 cup cooled green tea
- 2 cups spinach
- 1 cup pineapple chunks
- 1 scoop of protein powder
- 1 tbsp of chia seeds
- 5 ice cubes

Instructions

1) In a high-powered blender, combine all of the items, except the chia seeds.
2) To avoid chia seeds sticking to the blender container, add them towards the conclusion of the blending process.
3) If you like a thicker smoothie, add ice cubes and mix until the desired consistency is achieved.

2.31 Toasted Avocado with Egg

Ready in 13 min
Servings: 1
Difficulty: Easy
Ingredients

- 1 slice of toasted gluten-free bread
- 1 teaspoon of ghee
- 1/2 of an avocado
- 1 scrambled egg
- Red pepper flakes
- Handful of spinach

Instructions

1) Spread ghee on the gluten-free bread & toast it.
2) Place the avocado on the bread and spread it out evenly. Put additional spinach on top of the avocado, and then add a cooked or poached egg and a sprinkling of red pepper flakes to finish.
3) Serve open-faced with a knife and fork, or form a sandwich by adding an extra piece of bread.

2.32 Porridge of Chia Quinoa

Ready in 7 min
Servings: 2
Difficulty: Easy
Ingredients

- 1 cup cashew milk
- ¼ cup walnuts, toasted
- ½ teaspoon ground cinnamon
- 2 teaspoon raw honey
- 2 cups of quinoa, cooked
- 1 cup frozen blueberries
- 1 tbsp chia seeds

Instructions

1) In a saucepan, mix the quinoa & cashew milk and gently reheat over moderately low heat.
2) Toss in the blueberries, cinnamon, and walnuts and stir to combine. Remove the pan from the heat and add the raw honey. Chia seeds are sprinkled on top.
3) Toss in raw cacao nibs and serve in bowls for a boost of antioxidants.

2.33 Overnight Oats Pecan Banana Bread Recipe

Ready in 6 hrs. 15 min
Servings: 2
Difficulty: Easy

Ingredients

- 1/4 cup of fresh yogurt
- Banana slices, fig halves, honey, roasted pecans, and pomegranate seeds for serving
- 2 tbsp toasted coconut flakes
- 2 tbsp fresh honey
- 1 cup rolled oats
- 1 cup of milk
- 2 mashed bananas,
- 2 teaspoon vanilla extract
- 1 tbsp chia seeds
- 1/4 teaspoon of sea salt

Instructions

1) Combine the oats, milk, bananas, unsweetened coconut flakes, yogurt, honey, vanilla extract, chia seeds and sea salt in a medium mixing bowl. Pour the mixture into two dishes or glass jars. Refrigerate for at least six hours, preferably overnight after covering. Stir in the banana slices, toasted pecans, and fig halves, and serve warm if preferred. Pour with honey & pomegranate seeds to finish.

2.34 Smoothie with Greek yogurt for recovery

Ready in 15 min
Servings: 2
Difficulty: Easy
Ingredients

- 1 cup of nut milk
- pinch of ground cinnamon, pistachios, or cardamom, or bee pollen
- ½ cup of yogurt
- ¼ cup spinach
- 4 ice cubes
- ¼ cup frozen blueberries
- 1 tbsp nut butter

Instructions

1) In a blender, combine all ingredients and pulse until smooth.

2.35 Smoothie with Cacao and Berries

Ready in 10 min
Servings: 2
Difficulty: Easy
Ingredients

- 1 cup almond or coconut milk
- 1/2 cup water
- 3 tbsp cacao powder
- 1 tbsp honey
- Ice
- Cacao nibs
- 1 cup spinach
- 1 cup frozen raspberries
- 1 banana

Instructions

1) In a blender, combine all ingredients and mix until smooth. As desired, garnish with cocoa nibs. Take a drink and relax!

2.36 Turmeric Scramble with Nutrients

Ready in 10 min
Servings: 1
Difficulty: Easy
Ingredients

- 1 cayenne pepper
- 2 radishes grated
- 2 eggs
- 2 kale leaves
- 1 clove garlic
- 1 tbsp turmeric
- 2 tbsp coconut oil

Instructions

1) Lightly sauté garlic in a skillet with coconut oil.
2) Crack eggs & scramble them in a pan.

3) Adding the shredded kale, saffron, & cayenne when the eggs are nearly done.
4) Garnish with radish and sprouts and serve!

2.37 Breakfast with Chia and Raspberry

Ready in 30 min
Servings: 1
Difficulty: Easy
Ingredients
- 1 cup of frozen raspberries
- 3 tbsp of chia seeds
- 1 cup plant milk
- 1 pinch of vanilla
- 3 tbsp coconut

Instructions

1) In a bowl, mash all berries with a fork. Mix in the coconut, vanilla and chia seeds. Pour in the milk and stir to combine. Allow to soak for at least 30 mins or overnight inside the refrigerator. Top extra chia seeds, nut butter, fruit, and mint in a dish.

2.38 No-Bake Protein Turmeric Donuts

Ready in 45 min
Servings: 8
Difficulty: Easy
Ingredients
- 7 pieces dates
- 2 tbsp syrup of maple
- 1 tbsp of turmeric powder
- ¼ teaspoon of vanilla essence
- 1 teaspoon vanilla powder
- ¼ cup of shredded coconut
- ¼ cup dark chocolate
- 1½ cups of raw cashews

Instructions
1) In a food processor, combine all the ingredients (besides the chocolate) & mix on high till a sticky and smooth cookie forms.
2) Form mixture into 8 balls & press into donut mold made of silicone.
3) To set the mold, cover it in plastic wrap and lay it in the freezer for 30 minutes.
4) To make the chocolate coating, fill a pot halfway with water, then bring to a boil.
5) Set a smaller pan over the larger one and pour the chocolate into it. Gently stir even the chocolate has melted completely.
6) Once the donuts have been set, take them from the mold and coat them with the dark chocolate before storing them in a tight jar in the fridge.

2.39 Paleo Pancakes with Nutty Choco-Nana

Ready in 20 min
Servings: 10
Difficulty: Easy
Ingredients
- 2 teaspoon raw cacao powder
- 2 teaspoon creamy almond butter
- 1 tbsp pure vanilla extract
- Pinch of salt
- 2 eggs
- 2 bananas
- Coconut oil
- 4 tbsp raw cacao powder

Instructions
1) To make the chocolate sauce, first melted the coconut oil and then added the cacao powder. Set aside after mixing until thoroughly incorporated.
2) To make the pancakes, melt a tbsp of coconut oil in a large skillet over medium-low heat.

3) In a mixing bowl (or blender), combine all pancake ingredients & pulse on high till smooth.
4) Scoop the batter into a 14-cup measuring cup & pour onto the griddle to produce one pancake. Cook for 5 minutes before gently flipping over and cooking for two more minutes. Repeat until you've made 10 pancakes and all of the batters have gone.
5) Allow the pancakes to cool for 5 minutes before serving on a wire baking rack.
6) Pancakes may be stored in the refrigerator for up to 5 days or frozen for up to 30 days.

2.40 Breakfast Bars with Sweet Potatoes and Cranberries

Ready in 1 hr. 30 min
Servings: 16
Difficulty: Easy
Ingredients
- 1 ½ cups sweet potato
- ¼ cup of water
- 2 tbsp coconut oil
- 1 ½ teaspoon baking soda
- 1 cup cranberries
- 2 tbsp maple syrup
- 2 eggs
- 1 cup of almond meal
- ⅓ cup of coconut flour

Instructions
1) Preheat oven to 350 ° degrees Fahrenheit.
2) Mix the maple syrup, potatoes purée, melted coconut oil, water, & eggs in a large mixing bowl. Stir until everything is well blended.
3) Sift together the coconut flour, almond meal, & baking soda in another dish.
4) Combine the dry ingredients with the potato mixture & thoroughly combine.
5) Line the bottom of a 9-inch square baking sheet with parchment paper and grease it with coconut oil.

6) Pour the mixture into the prepared baking pan & level the top, and fill in the corners with a moist spatula. Place cranberries on the top and press them down.
7) Bake for 40 minutes, till a toothpick inserted near the center, comes out clean. Please remove it from the pan & cut it into squares once it has cooled fully.

2.41 Turmeric Scones for anti Inflammation

Ready in 35 min
Servings: 6
Difficulty: Easy
Ingredients
- 1/4 cup of arrowroot flour
- 1 tbsp of coconut flour
- 1 egg
- 1/4 cup of red palm oil
- 3 tbsp maple syrup
- 1 teaspoon turmeric
- 1/2 teaspoon black pepper
- Pinch of salt
- 1 teaspoon vanilla extract
- 1 cup of almond flour
- 1 cup of almonds

Instructions
1) Preheat the oven to 350 degrees Fahrenheit.
2) In a food processor, coarsely chop almonds. Combine the chopped almonds and the remaining dry ingredients in a mixing bowl and fluff with a fork.

3) In a separate bowl, whisk together the syrup, egg, oil, and vanilla extract; add to the dry ingredients. Mix until everything is well incorporated, then move the dough on a cutting board or even a plastic-wrapped countertop. Cut into sixths after patting into a spherical form about one inch thick.

4) Bake for 20 minutes in a preheated oven and until a tester placed in the middle comes out clean.

2.42 Muffins with Chocolate Avocado and Blueberries

Ready in 18 min
Servings: 9
Difficulty: Easy
Ingredients

- 1/3 cup of coconut sugar
- ¼ teaspoon salt
- 2 eggs
- ¼ cup blueberries
- 2 tbsp dark chocolate chips
- 1 ripe avocado
- 1/4 cup of raw cacao powder
- 1 cup of almond flour
- ½ cup almond milk
- 2 teaspoon baking powder
- 2 tbsp coconut flour

Instructions

1) Preheat the oven to 375 degrees Fahrenheit. Grease a muffin tray with coconut oil or use muffin liners.

2) In a blender, combine the eggs, avocado, sugar, and salt, along with 1 tablespoon cacao powder. Mix on high until the avocado is completely broken down as well as the sauce has the consistency of silky custard.

3) Sift together 14 cups icing sugar, baking soda, coconut flour, and almond flour in a small basin.

4) Slowly fold in the dry ingredients after adding some almond milk to a liquid

mixture. Mix only until everything is incorporated.

5) Combine the blueberries & chocolate chips in a mixing bowl.

6) Pour batter into prepared muffin tins, evenly dividing batter among 9 holes.

7) Bake for 18 minutes, till a toothpick injected in the middle comes out clean.

8) Take the muffins from the pan and let them cool on a wire rack.

9) Keep refrigerated for up to one week or frozen for up to 1 month.

2.43 Smoothie with raspberries and grapefruit

Ready in 15 min
Servings: 1
Difficulty: Easy
Ingredients

1) 1 pink grapefruit, Juice
2) 1 cup frozen raspberries
3) 1 frozen banana

Instructions

1) In a blender, combine all of the ingredients and mix until smooth.

2.44 Shroom Iced- Mocha

Ready in 5 min
Servings: 1
Difficulty: Easy
Ingredients

- 1 packet of Mushroom Coffee
- 1 teaspoon coconut oil
- ½ tbsp of cacao powder
- 8 oz hot water
- ½ cup almond milk
- ice cubes

Instructions

1) Dissolve the Four Sigmatic package in boiling water. Allow 2 minutes to cool after stirring to dissolve the powder.

2) Dissolve the coconut oil & cacao powder in a separate bowl.

3) Pour almond milk over coffee, top with ice, and enjoy!

2.45 Pancakes with a Savory Flavor

Ready in 25 min
Servings: 2
Difficulty: Easy
Ingredients

- ½ teaspoon of Chili Powder
- ¼ teaspoon Turmeric Powder
- ¼ teaspoon ground black pepper
- ½ chopped red onion
- 1 cilantro leaves chopped
- 1 serrano pepper minced
- 1/2-inch ginger
- fat of choice uses enough to shallow fry
- ½ cup of Almond Flour
- ½ cup of Tapioca Flour
- 1 cup Coconut Milk canned
- 1 teaspoon salt

Instructions
Making Batter
1) In a mixing dish, combine tapioca flour, coconut milk, almond flour, and spices.
2) Add onion, cilantro, serrano pepper, and ginger after that.

Fry Pancakes
1) Preheat a sauté pan over low-medium heat, add enough oil/fat to coat the pan and pour 14 cups of batter into the pan. Pour the ingredients into your pan and spread it out evenly.
2) Cook for 3-4 minutes on each side, drizzling a little additional oil on top of the pancake after flipping. (Stoves vary, so fry until golden brown on both sides.)
3) Keep adding oil as required until the batter is finished.
4) Serve with Paleo ketchup or green chutney.

2.46 Chia Pudding with Dark Chocolate and Orange

Ready in 3 hrs.
Servings: 2
Difficulty: Easy
Ingredients

- 1/3 cup chia seeds
- 3 tbsp cacao powder
- 1 cup of water
- Orange peel
- 1/4 cup of orange juice
- 1 tbsp orange zest
- 1 tbsp honey

Instructions
1) Mix the chia seeds, orange juice, orange zest, raw cacao powder, & honey in a large mixing dish. Mix thoroughly.
2) Stir in the water until all of the cacao powder has dissolved.
3) Cover the bowl with plastic wrap and refrigerate for at least 3 hours until chia seeds completely soaked all of the liquid. The chia pudding must have a thick consistency.
4) Pour the chia pudding into two glasses, top with orange peel and serve.

2.47 Smoothie Bowl with Tropical Turmeric

Ready in 15 min
Servings: 2
Difficulty: Easy
Ingredients

- 1 cup of orange juice
- 1 cup frozen pineapple
- Turmeric
- 1 cup frozen mango
- ½ banana
- 1 tbsp of chia

For Topping

- Strawberries sliced
- Coconut flakes
- Kiwis' slices
- Almonds chopped

Instructions

1) In a blender, combine all of the ingredients in the order stated. Blend until the mixture is smooth and creamy. If the mixture becomes too thick, you may need to add a dash of orange juice. Fruit slices, nuts, and coconut flakes may be sprinkled over the top.

2.48 Breakfast with Smoked Salmon & Spinach

Ready in 30 min
Servings: 4
Difficulty: Easy
Ingredients
- 1 garlic clove
- 1/2 teaspoon onion powder
- 1/2 teaspoon garlic powder
- ½ sliced onion
- 1/2 cup of mushrooms
- 2 cups of spinach
- 1/4 teaspoon paprika
- 2 tbsp ghee
- 2 tbsp olive oil
- Sea salt & ground black pepper
- 4 eggs
- 8 oz. sliced smoked salmon
- 2 peeled sweet potatoes

Instructions

1) Preheat the oven to 425 degrees Fahrenheit.
2) Dice the potatoes and season to taste with olive oil, onion powder, garlic powder, and paprika.
3) Arrange the potato on a baking tray and bake for 25 minutes, rotating halfway through.
4) Over high heat, bring a saucepan of water to the boil.
5) Place the eggs in the boiling water, cover, and simmer for 7 minutes.

6) Take the water and rinse the eggs under cold water; peel your eggs and keep them aside.
7) Add the onion and garlic to the melted ghee over medium-high heat.
8) Cook for another 1 to 2 minutes before adding the sliced mushrooms.
9) Season to taste, then simmer for another 5 minutes, or until everything is soft.
10) Mix the spinach and simmer for 2 minutes, or until wilted.
11) Toss the potatoes with the spinach-mushroom mix, an egg, and smoked salmon slices before serving.

2.49 Avocado Buns for a Keto Breakfast Burger

Ready in 20 min
Servings: 1
Difficulty: Easy
Ingredients
- 1 ripe avocado
- 1 tomato
- 1 lettuce leaf
- 1 tbsp Paleo mayonnaise
- 1 egg
- 2 bacon rashers
- 1 red onion slice
- Sea salt
- Sesame seeds

Instructions

1) In a chilly frying pan, place the bacon rashers. Start cooking the bacon after the stove is turned on. Flip the bacon with a fork when it begins to curl. Cook the bacon till it has become crispy.
2) Take the bacon from the pan and break the egg into it, cooking it in the same pan with the bacon grease. Cook until the yolk remains liquid, but the white is set.
3) Cut the avocados in halves horizontally. Remove the pit by scooping out of its covering using a spoon.

4) Use Paleo mayonnaise to fill the hole in which the pit used to be.
5) Add lettuce, tomato, onion, bacon, and a fried egg to the top layer. Season with a pinch of salt.
6) Add the second part of the avocado on top. Sesame seeds may be sprinkled on top.

2.50 Avocado Egg with Prosciutto Wrapping

Ready in 15 min
Servings: 2
Difficulty: Easy
Ingredients

- 2 avocados
- Salt & pepper
- 6 slices of prosciutto
- 2 tbsp olive oil
- Tomato slices
- Chopped parsley
- 2 eggs

Instructions
1) Prepare a medium saucepan of water to a moderate simmer over low heat.
2) Line a small bowl with food-safe plastic wrap and drizzle it with olive oil.
3) Crack one egg into the prepared dish, fold the plastic wrap in half, and make a knot. 3 minutes in the boiling water with the wrapped egg Rep with the second egg.
4) Take the eggs out of the water and place them on a tray. Gently detach the eggs from the plastic wrap by cutting them apart. After that, please remove it from the equation.
5) Flatten the prosciutto slices with the back of a knife before serving.
6) Cut the avocado in half and peel away the outer membrane. Scoop out the avocado's center to make almost the same proportion as the fried egg.

Carefully place the egg in and wrap the avocado over it on both sides.
7) Wrap two pieces of prosciutto horizontally and one-piece vertically around the sealed avocado. Carry on with the second egg in the same manner.
8) Fry a prosciutto-wrapped avocado with olive oil for approximately 10 minutes over medium heat, beginning with the loose bacon ends. Turn the bacon regularly until it is crispy all across.
9) Drain any extra oil on such a paper towel before serving. Sprinkle salt, pepper, and chopped parsley over the filled avocado. Serves with tomato slices on the side.

2.51 Chickpea and Cauliflower Tikka Masala

Ready in 20 min
Servings: 4
Difficulty: Easy
Ingredients

- 4 cups of cauliflower florets
- ¼ teaspoon of salt
- Fresh cilantro for garnish
- ¼ cup water
- 1 can rinsed chickpeas
- 1 1/2 cups tikka masala sauce
- 2 tbsp butter
- 1 tbsp coconut oil

Instructions
1) In a large skillet, heat the oil over medium-high heat. Cook, occasionally tossing, until cauliflower is lightly browned, approximately 2 minutes. Add the water, cover, and simmer for 5 minutes or when the cauliflower is soft. Cook for 2 minutes until chickpeas and sauce are heated. Remove the pan from the heat and add the butter. If desired, garnish with cilantro.

2.52 Turkey Stuffed Peppers in the Air Fryer

Ready in 30 min
Servings: 3
Difficulty: Easy
Ingredients

- 3 red bell peppers
- 1 tbsp olive oil
- ¼ teaspoon pepper
- ¼ cup grated Parmesan
- ¼ cup shredded mozzarella cheese
- 12 ounces of ground turkey
- ½ cup brown rice, cooked
- 3 tbsp flat-leaf parsley, finely chopped
- ¼ cup of breadcrumbs
- ¾ cup marinara sauce

Instructions

1) Spray the air fryer basket with cooking spray. Remove the tops of the peppers and set them aside. Remove the seeds from the peppers and keep them aside.

2) In a large skillet, heat the oil over medium-high heat. Cook, occasionally tossing, until turkey is browned, approximately 4 minutes. Cook, tossing periodically until rice and panko are warmed through, approximately 1 minute. Remove the pan from the heat and add the marinara, parsley, pepper, and Parmesan cheese. Distribute the mixture equally among the peppers that have been prepped.

3) Put the peppers in an air-fryer basket that has been prepared. Place the pepper top in the basket's bottom. Cook for approximately 8 minutes at 350 degrees F, just until the peppers become soft. Cook for a further 2 minutes, or until the mozzarella is melted.

Chapter 3: Lunch Recipes

3.1 Fruit Salad with Red, White, and Blueberries

Ready in 40 min
Servings: 8
Difficulty: Easy
Ingredients

- 1-pint strawberries
- 2 tbsp lemon juice
- 4 bananas
- 1-pint blueberries
- ½ cup white sugar

Instructions

1) In a mixing bowl, combine the strawberries and blueberries, season with sugar & lemon juice, and toss gently. Refrigerate for at least 30 minutes or until completely cool. Divide bananas into 3/4-inch slices and combine with the berries about 20 minutes before serving.

3.2 Seared Salmon in a Pan

Ready in 20 min
Servings: 4
Difficulty: Easy
Ingredients

- ⅛ teaspoon salt
- ⅛ teaspoon ground black pepper
- 4 slices of lemon
- 4 fillets salmon
- 2 tbsp olive oil
- 2 tbsp capers

Instructions

1) Preheat a big heavy skillet for 3 minutes over medium heat.
2) Olive oil should be used to coat the salmon. Increase the heat to high in the skillet. 3 minutes in the oven Season with salt and pepper and capers. Cook for 5 minutes on the other side, or until browned. When a fork easily flakes the salmon, it's done.
3) Arrange the salmon on separate dishes and serve with lemon slices as a garnish

3.3 Broccoli Roasted with Ease

Ready in 30 min
Servings: 4
Difficulty: Easy
Ingredients

- 14 ounces of broccoli
- salt and black pepper
- 1 tbsp of olive oil

Instructions

1) Preheat oven to 425 degrees Fahrenheit.
2) Step 2: Separate the florets from the stem of the broccoli. Slice the stalk into 1/4-inch segments after peeling it. In a mixing bowl, combine florets & stem portions with olive oil; move to a baking tray and season with salt.
3) Roast for 18 minutes in an oven and bake until broccoli is cooked & lightly browned.

3.4 Salad with Tomatoes and Avocados

Ready in 15 min
Servings: 4
Difficulty: Easy
Ingredients

- ½ cup of balsamic vinegar
- 1 teaspoon of Dijon mustard
- ¼ cup virgin olive oil
- 2 small tomatoes
- 1 pinch black pepper
- 1 peeled avocado

Instructions

1) Whisk together all the mustard, balsamic vinegar, olive oil, and pepper in a small basin. Set the pieces of avocado & tomato alternately on a large serving plate or individual plates, as if they were spokes of a wheel. Serve immediately with a thin drizzle of dressing.

3.5 Peppers grilled

Ready in 15 min
Servings: 6
Difficulty: Easy
Ingredients

- 1 pinch oregano
- 1 cup mozzarella cheese
- 3 green bell peppers
- ½ cup of sliced jalapeno peppers

Instructions

1) Preheat the grill to medium-high heat. Lightly oil the grill grate once it's heated.
2) Arrange the pepper slices on the grill so that the insides are facing down. Cook for 3 to 5 minutes, or until slightly charred.

3) Flip the peppers over and top with jalapeño slices. Add some mozzarella cheese and a pinch of oregano on the top. Remove to a platter and serve after the cheese has melted.

3.6 Italian Style Mushrooms with Spinach

Ready in 30 min
Servings: 4
Difficulty: Easy
Ingredients

- 2 cloves garlic
- ½ cup of white wine
- salt and black pepper to taste
- chopped fresh parsley
- 4 tbsp olive oil
- 14 ounces sliced mushrooms
- 10 ounces fresh spinach
- 2 tbsp balsamic vinegar
- 1 small onion

Instructions

1) In a large pan, heat the olive oil over medium-high heat. In a skillet, sauté the onion and garlic until they begin to soften. Fry the mushrooms for 3 to 4 minutes, or till they begin to shrink. Toss within spinach and cook for a minute, stirring regularly, or until the spinach has wilted.
2) Stir in the vinegar until it is completely absorbed, then add the white wine. Reduce to a low heat setting and continue to cook till the wine has nearly fully absorbed. Season to taste with salt and pepper, then top with fresh parsley. Serve immediately.

3.7 Turmeric Milk

Ready in 15 min **Servings:** 1 **Difficulty** Easy
Ingredients

- 1 cup almond milk
- 1 piece fresh turmeric root
- 1 piece fresh ginger root
- 1 tbsp honey
- 1 pinch ground cinnamon
- 1 pinch ground turmeric

Instructions

1) In a mixing bowl, combine the turmeric root, ginger root, and honey, smashing the turmeric & ginger as much as possible.
2) In a pan over medium heat, warm the almond milk. Medium heats after little bubbles appear around the edges. Allow around 2 tbsp of milk to soften the turmeric mixture and the honey to dissolve into such a paste-like consistency.
3) In a saucepan, combine the turmeric paste and milk; reduce to medium-low heat and simmer, constantly stirring, until entirely blended. For a smooth texture, use an immersion blender.
4) Fill a cup halfway with turmeric tea and sprinkle with ground turmeric & cinnamon.

3.8 Dark Chocolate Melt-In-Your-Mouth Homemade

Ready in 1 hr 10 min
Servings: 8
Difficulty: Easy
Ingredients

- 3 tbsp honey
- ½ teaspoon of vanilla extract
- ½ cup of coconut oil
- ½ cup of cocoa powder

Instructions

1) In a pan with butter, gently melt coconut oil. In a large mixing bowl, combine cocoa powder, honey, & vanilla extract. Fill a candy mold or a pliable tray halfway with the mixture. Refrigerate for 1 hour or until completely cooled.

3.9 Smoothie with cherries and coconut

Ready in 10 min **Servings:** 2 **Difficulty:**Easy
Ingredients

- 1 cup cherries
- ½ cup of almond milk
- ½ cup of coconut water
- 1 cup of ice

Instructions

1) In a blender, combine cherries, almond milk, ice, & coconut water until smooth.

3.10 Smoothie with Mighty Melon and Green Tea

Ready in 10 min
Servings: 2
Difficulty: Easy
Ingredients

- 1 cup of cantaloupe chunks
- 1 pear
- ½ cup plain yogurt
- 1 cup chilled green tea
- 1 cup pineapple chunks
- 4 fresh mint leaves

Instructions

1) In a blender, combine the tea, cantaloupe, pineapple, yogurt, pear, and mint leaves. Blend until completely smooth.

3.11 Tuna Steaks with Grape & Caper Salsa on the Grill

Ready in 25 min
Servings: 4
Difficulty: Easy
Ingredients

- 1 shallot
- 4 tuna steaks
- ¼ cup lemon juice
- 2 tbsp chopped parsley
- 1 tbsp olive oil
- salt and black pepper
- 2 cups of red seedless grapes
- ⅓ cup of capers

Instructions

1) Preheat an outside grill over medium-high heat and brush the grate liberally with oil.
2) In a mixing bowl, combine the capers, parsley, grapes, shallot, & olive oil; season with salt and pepper to taste, and leave aside. Brush tuna steaks with lemon juice and place on a platter. To taste, season with salt.
3) Cook tuna steaks on a hot grill until the desired doneness is reached, about 2 to 3 minutes on each side for medium-rare. Toss with the grape & caper salsa before serving.

3.12 Life Juice with Turmeric and Ginger

Ready in 5 min
Servings: 1
Difficulty: Easy
Ingredients

- ½ lemon
- 1 piece ginger
- ½ teaspoon turmeric
- 2 Fuji apples
- 1 orange

Instructions

1) Using a juicer, juice the apples, orange, lemon, & ginger; whisk in the turmeric until it is uniformly distributed.

3.13 Turmeric Chicken Stew

Ready in 43 min
Servings: 6
Difficulty: Easy
Ingredients

- ½ red onion
- 2 teaspoons turmeric
- ½ cup chicken broth
- 1 small eggplant
- 2 cloves garlic
- 2 tbsp olive oil
- 2 chicken breasts
- 2 sweet potatoes
- 1 tbsp minced ginger root

Instructions

1) In a large pan, heat the olive oil over medium-high heat. Cook, occasionally stirring, until the chicken is browned and so no longer pink, mostly in the middle, approximately 5 minutes. Continue cooking until sweet potatoes & onion are transparent, about 2 to 3 minutes. Cook for another minute, or until the eggplant, garlic, ginger, & turmeric are aromatic. Pour in the broth and cook, stirring periodically, until the stew has thickened, approximately 20 minutes.

3.14 Salad with Salmon and Avocado

Ready in 35 min
Servings: 4
Difficulty: Easy
Ingredients

- salt and pepper
- 4 ounces fresh mushrooms
- 2 fillets salmon
- ¼ cup butter
- 8 ounces leaf lettuce
- 1 avocado
- 12 grape tomatoes
- 2 tbsp olive oil
- 2 tbsp distilled white vinegar
- 1 ounce feta cheese
- 5 sprigs of fresh cilantro
- 1 fresh jalapeno pepper

Instructions
1) Preheat the broiler in the oven. Aluminum foil should be used to line a baking pan. Brush the salmon with 2 tbsp of butter before placing it on the foil. Salt & pepper to taste. Broil for 15 minutes or until the salmon flakes easily with a fork.
2) In a pan over medium heat, melt the leftover butter and sauté the mushrooms until soft.
3) Toss the tomatoes with 1 tbsp oil in a mixing basin. Salt & pepper to taste.
4) Toss the mushrooms, lettuce, avocado, tomatoes, cilantro, salmon, and jalapeño in a large mixing bowl. Drizzle the remaining olive oil and vinegar over the top. To serve, sprinkle with salt and black pepper and top with feta cheese.

3.15 Chickpea salad & Tuna

Ready in 10 min
Servings: 4
Difficulty: Easy
Ingredients

- 1 can of black olives
- salt and black pepper
- ¼ cup Italian parsley
- 1 can Italian tuna in olive oil
- 1 can chickpeas
- ¼ cup cheese,
- ½ red onion
- Lemon juice

Instructions

1) In a mixing bowl, combine the tuna, olives, chickpeas, red onion, lemon juice, parsley, & feta cheese. Salt & pepper to taste.

3.16 Salad of Heirloom Tomatoes with Rosemary

Ready in 20 min
Servings: 4
Difficulty: Easy
Ingredients

- 1 sprig of fresh rosemary
- ⅛ teaspoon oregano
- ¼ cup virgin olive oil
- 2 tbsp rice wine vinegar
- 3 heirloom tomatoes
- 3 heirloom tomatoes
- Salt & black pepper

Instructions

1) In a large mixing bowl, combine the olive oil, rosemary, rice wine vinegar, & oregano. Toss in the tiny and big tomatoes until they are equally covered. Refrigerate for 10 to 15 minutes, covered and cooled. Salt & black pepper to taste. Before serving, toss one more

3.17 Salad with strawberries and spinach

Ready in 1 hr 10 min
Servings: 4
Difficulty: Easy
Ingredients
- ½ cup of white sugar
- ½ cup of olive oil
- ¼ cup distilled vinegar
- 2 tbsp sesame seeds
- 1 tbsp poppy seeds
- ¼ teaspoon paprika
- 10 ounces spinach
- 1-quart strawberries
- ¼ teaspoon of Worcestershire sauce
- 1 tbsp minced onion
- ¼ cup almonds

Instructions
1) Combine the sesame seeds, sugar, olive oil, poppy seeds, vinegar, Worcestershire sauce, paprika, and onion in a medium mixing bowl. Refrigerate for one hour, covered.
2) Combine the spinach, strawberries, and almonds in a large mixing basin. Toss the salad with the dressing. Before serving, chill for 10 to 15 minutes.

3.18 Spanish Mackerel, broiled

Ready in 15 min
Servings: 6
Difficulty: Easy
Ingredients
- ½ teaspoon of paprika
- salt and black pepper
- 12 slices of lemon
- 6 fillets Spanish mackerel fillets
- ¼ cup of olive oil

Instructions
1) Place the oven rack approximately 6 inches from the heat source and preheat the broiler. Lubricate a baking dish lightly.
2) Rub each mackerel fillet on both sides with olive oil and lay the skin side down in the baking dish. Season the paprika, salt, & pepper to taste on each fillet. Two lemon slices should be placed on top of each fillet.
3) Broil the fillets for 5 to 7 minutes, just until the fish just starts to flake. Serve right away.

3.19 Big Fat Greek Salad

Ready in 1 hr 10 min
Servings: 4
Difficulty: Easy
Ingredients
- 2 cups of cherry tomatoes
- ¼ red onion
- ½ red bell pepper
- 2 large cucumbers
- 1 pinch of salt
- 2 tbsp minced oregano
- salt and black pepper
- 1 pinch cayenne pepper
- ½ cup pitted Kalamata olives
- ½ cup green olives
- 1 package feta cheese
- 1 teaspoon oregano
- ¼ cup of red wine vinegar
- ⅓ cup olive oil

Instructions
1) Using only a channel knife, create a striped pattern by peeling off just a few strips of cucumbers skin. Cucumbers should be cut in half crosswise. Before chopping into 1/4- to 1/2-inch slices, divide each half into quarters. Toss with kosher salt in a colander and set aside for 15 minutes.

2) Meanwhile, halve the cherry tomatoes. Cucumbers should be rinsed and drained completely for another 10 to 15 minutes.
3) While the cucumbers are draining, finely slice the onion. Bell pepper should be cut into strips. Slice strips in diamond-shaped pieces by turning the knife diagonally. Kalamata and green olives, sliced
4) In a mixing dish, combine the cucumbers, bell pepper, onion, olives, tomatoes, & 2 teaspoons oregano. Salt, black pepper & cayenne pepper to taste. Toss in the vinegar and toss again. Drizzle some olive oil on top. Mix in 2/3 of the feta cheese & toss once more. Refrigerate for 60 minutes after wrapping in plastic wrap.
5) Toss the salad one more. Season with salt and pepper to taste. Sprinkle the remaining feta cheese over the top and finish with the oregano.

3.20 Salad with Chicken, Avocado, & Goat Cheese on Spinach

Ready in 20 min
Servings: 4
Difficulty: Easy
Ingredients
- 1 cup cherry tomatoes
- 1 ½ cups cooked chicken
- ¼ cup nuts
- 8 cups spinach
- ⅓ cup goat cheese
- 1 avocado
- ½ cup of corn kernels

Dressing of Salad
- 3 tbsp white wine vinegar
- 2 tbsp extra-virgin olive oil
- 1 tbsp Dijon mustard
- 1 pinch salt and black pepper

Instructions
1) In a small skillet, heat the oil over medium-high heat. 3 to 5 minutes in a heated pan, toast pine nuts until lightly browned & aromatic.
2) Toss spinach with pine nuts, tomatoes, avocado, corn kernels, chicken, & goat cheese in a large salad dish.
3) In a small bowl, whisk together olive oil, white wine vinegar, & Dijon mustard until smooth; add salt and pepper. Toss the salad gently in the dressing to coat it.

3.21 Salmon Patties with Butternut Squash

Ready in 40 min
Servings: 10 Patties
Difficulty: Easy
Ingredients
- 1/2 C. Butternut Squash
- 24 oz Canned Salmon
- 4 Eggs
- ¼ Coconut Flour
- 1/4 Green Onion
- 1 tbsp Coconut Aminos
- 2 teaspoon Dijon Mustard
- 1 teaspoon Garlic Powder
- Salt & Pepper

Instructions
1) Preheat oven to 375 ° F. Using parchment paper or a silicone mat, line a baking sheet.
2) Combine all ingredients in a large mixing basin and stir until well blended.
3) Divide the mixture into ten portions that are about equal in size. Each portion should be rolled into a ball but then pressed into a 1-inch-thick patty on the baking sheet. Rep till all of the concoction has been consumed.
4) Preheat oven to 350°F and bake patties for 25-30 min, or until firm.
5) Optional Step: Brown the patty in a pan with 1 tbsp of coconut oil over medium heat.

3.22 Sweet Potato Fries

Ready in 30 min
Servings: 5
Difficulty: Easy
Ingredients
- 3 Sweet Potatoes
- Garlic Powder
- Salt and black pepper
- 2 tbsp Avocado Oil

Instructions
1) Sweet potatoes should be peeled and sliced into 1/4-½ inch thick fries.
2) Optional Step: To eliminate the starch, soak the fries in a dish of ice water for approximately 30 minutes. Rinse the fries and pat them dry.
3) Combine the fries, paprika, garlic powder, black pepper, & oil in a large mixing basin. Toss until the oil and spices are well distributed among the fries. Arrange the fries on the baking pan in an equal layer.
4) Fries should be baked for 15 minutes. Fries should be flipped. Bake for a further 10-15 minutes, or until the edges are gently browned.
5) Add the sea salt after the fries are done. Enjoy.

3.23 Sandwich with Smashed Chickpea Avocado Salad & Cranberries + Lemon

Ready in 5 min
Servings: 2
Difficulty: Easy
Ingredients
- 2 teaspoon lemon juice
- 1/4 cup cranberries
- salt & pepper
- 1 - 15 oz can chickpeas
- 1 ripe avocado

Instructions
1) Using a fork, mash chickpeas in a medium bowl. Add in the avocado and crush it with a fork until it is smooth but still has a few lumpy chunks.
2) Add the cranberries and lemon juice. To taste, season with salt. Keep refrigerated until ready to use (best within 1-2 days).
3) To serve, toast the bread and spread 1/2 of the chickpea avocado salad on one piece. If preferred, garnish with arugula, red onion, or spinach. Top with the second toasted slice, now cut in half & enjoy!

3.24 No Mayo Mediterranean Tuna Salad

Ready in 20 min
Servings: 6
Difficulty: Easy
Ingredients
- 1/2 red onion
- 1 cup of roasted red peppers
- 1/2 cup of pepperoncini
- 2 cans Albacore Tuna
- 1/4 cup feta cheese
- olives
- 1/3 cup parsley
- Sundried tomatoes
- 1 14.5 ounces can chickpeas
- 1/2 avocado
- Pinch of fine sea salt
- Pinch of black pepper
- 1 cucumber
- 2 teaspoons capers
- 1 teaspoon lemon juice
- 1 teaspoon dried parsley
- Red Wine Vinaigrette
- 2 tbsp olive oil
- Pinch of salt
- Pinch of black pepper
- 2 tbsp red wine vinegar
- 1 teaspoon oregano, dried

Instructions

1) Mix all of the salad components in a large mixing basin.
2) Whisk together the dressing ingredients in a small dish.
3) Toss the ingredients in the dressing to mix.
4) Taste and adjust the seasonings as needed!
5) End up serving over a salad, over a sandwich, with spaghetti, lettuce wraps, or half an avocado.

3.25 Greek Salad Chicken Wrap

Ready in 45 min
Servings: 4
Difficulty: Easy
Ingredients
For Greek Salad

- 4 cups romaine
- 1/3 cup cherry tomatoes
- 1/4 cup red onion
- 1/2 cup cucumber slices
- 4 tbsp kalamata olives
- 1/2 cup cheese
- 1 tbsp red wine vinegar
- 1 tbsp olive oil
- fresh lemon wedges
- 4 whole wheats
- 1/2 cup of prepared hummus

For chicken

- 2 chicken breasts
- 1 1/2 teaspoons olive oil

Few shakes of the following per chicken breast

- garlic powder
- lemon pepper
- dried oregano

Instructions

1) Preheat the oven to 375 ° F for the chicken. Spray a baking pan with cooking spray and line it with foil. Season 2 bone-in chicken breasts with salt, pepper, dried oregano, and lemon pepper and place on top. Drizzle 1 1/2 tbsp of olive oil over the chicken and bake about 35-40 minutes, or until cooked through. Use right away or save the leftovers for such a wrap. This amount of chicken will make four big wraps.
2) To create the salad, cut the romaine lettuce and set it in a bowl. Cherry tomatoes, olives, red onion, cucumbers, and feta cheese are sprinkled over the top. Add a couple of shakes of dry oregano on top. Drizzle with vinegar & olive oil to finish. Squeeze a juicy lemon over everything (1 large wedge is fine). Stir in the spices and taste to see if they need to be adjusted.
3) To prepare the wrap, put 2 tbsp of hummus on your preferred wrap. Top with chicken pieces and a hearty helping of Greek salad. Wrap, roll and eat.

3.26 Avocado Sauced Grilled Salmon Taco Wraps

Ready in 20 min
Servings: 4
Difficulty: Easy
Ingredients

- 1/4 cup Avocado Sauce
- 1 head of butter lettuce
- 1 orange
- 2 cups pre-packaged coleslaw mix
- 1 lime juice
- 2 tbsp Seasoning Salt
- 2 fresh salmon filets
- 2 tbsp olive oil

Instructions

1) Make the Everyday Seasoning Salt & Avocado Sauce ahead of time to save time
2) Season salmon with Seasoning Salt liberally. Drizzle just slight olive oil over each fillet to help it stick together.
3) Preheat the grill to normal high heat.

Grill the salmon for 5 to 8 minutes on each side, rotating once. Cook until the fillets are easy to flake but still juicy. Remove the steaks from the grill and put them aside to cool.

4) Mix Cole slaw mix with chopped cilantro leaves & 1 lime juice in a small mixing dish. season with salt to taste

5) Rinse the butter lettuce leaves and dry them in a salad spinner or with paper towels. To make lettuce wrap tacos, use the nicest cup-shaped leaves.

6) Cooled salmon fillets should be broken apart. Place salmon slices into lettuce wrap tacos and top with Coleslaw dressing.

7) Add a hearty dab of Avocado Sauce to each lettuce wrap taco.

3.27 Bowls of Turkey Taco Meal Prep

Ready in 1 hr 10 min
Servings: 4
Difficulty: Easy
Ingredients
For Rice
- ⅛ teaspoon of salt
- 1 lime
- ¾ cup brown rice

Turkey
- ¾ lb. lean ground turkey
- 2 tbsp homemade taco seasoning
- ⅔ cup of water

Salsa
- ¼ cup red onion
- ½ lime juice
- 1 pint cherry tomatoes

- 1 chopped jalapeno
- ⅛ teaspoon of salt

Other
- 12 oz can corn kernels
- ½ cup mozzarella

Instructions

1) Brown rice should be cooked according to package guidelines, with lime zest and salt added to the cooking water. Allow cooling gently before dividing into portions.

2) Cook until the turkey is no longer pink in a medium skillet over medium heat, splitting it up with a spatula (approximately 10 minutes).

3) The taco seasoning should be sprinkled over cooked meat before adding the water. Stir and cook for a few minutes or until the sauce has thickened.

4) Remove from the heat and set aside to cool gently before serving.

5) Toss together all of the salsa ingredients.

6) Divide the ingredients equally among four 2-cup size meal prep containers to make the lunch bowls.

3.28 Glowing Spiced Lentil Soup

Ready in 20 min
Servings: 7 Cups
Difficulty: Easy
Ingredients
- 2 garlic cloves
- 2 teaspoons turmeric
- 1 1/2 teaspoons cumin
- 1/2 teaspoon cinnamon
- 1 1/2 tbsp virgin olive oil
- 2 cups onion
- 1/4 teaspoon cardamom
- 3/4 cup uncooked red lentils
- 3 1/2 cups low-sodium vegetable broth
- 1 can diced tomatoes
- 1 can full-fat coconut milk
- 1/2 teaspoon fine sea sal

- Black pepper
- 1 spinach
- 2 teaspoons lime juice
- Red pepper flakes

Instructions

1) Combine the oil, onion, & garlic in a big saucepan. Add a bit of salt, stir, and cook for 4 to 5 minutes over medium heat until the onion softens.
2) Combine the turmeric, cumin, cinnamon, & cardamom in a large mixing bowl. Cook for another minute or so until aromatic.
3) Add the chopped tomatoes, coconut milk, red lentils, broth, salt, & pepper to taste. Taste and season with red pepper flakes. To blend, stir everything together. Raise the heat to high & bring the mixture to a low boil.
4) Reduce heat to medium-high and continue to cook, uncovered, for 18 to 22 minutes, or until the lentils remain bubbly and soft.
5) Remove the pan from the heat and whisk in the spinach once it has wilted. To taste, add the lime juice. If desired, season with extra salt and pepper. Garnish with toasted bread & lime wedges, ladled into bowls.

3.29 Pasta with Golden Sun-Dried Tomatoes and Red Lentils

Ready in 40 min
Servings: 6
Difficulty: Easy

Ingredients
- 6 cloves garlic
- 1 tbsp dried basil
- 1 tbsp dried oregano
- 1/4 cup virgin olive oil
- 1 sweet onion
- 2 teaspoons turmeric

- salt and pepper
- 1 tbsp apple cider vinegar
- 1 box red lentil pasta
- 1 can fire-roasted tomatoes
- 1/2 cup oil-packed sun-dried tomatoes
- 2 large spinach
- grated parmesan, nutritional yeast, seeds for topping

Instructions

1) In a large saucepan over medium heat, heat the olive oil. When the oil begins to shimmer, add the onion & simmer for 5-10 minutes, or until tender and caramelized. Garlic, basil, turmeric, salt, oregano, and pepper are added. Cook for 1 minute or until the mixture is aromatic. Slowly pour in the tomatoes and their juices, smashing the tomatoes with the back of a wooden spoon as you go. Toss in the sun-dried tomatoes & balsamic vinegar. Simmer for 10-15 minutes, or until the sauce has somewhat reduced. You may purée the sauce in a blender if desired.
2) Cook for another five minutes after adding the spinach.
3) Now, put a large pot of salted water to such a boil & cook the pasta until al dente, as directed on the box. Drain.
4) Toss the pasta with a liberal quantity of sauce in each bowl. Cheese, nuts, and herbs may be added as desired.

3.30 Glow getter Roasted Carrots Butternut Squash Soup

Ready in 40 min
Servings: 4
Difficulty: Easy
Ingredients
- ½ cup shallots
- 2 tbsp avocado oil
- 4 cup of vegetable stock
- 1 teaspoon salt
- Black pepper

- 1 can coconut milk
- 1-pound carrots
- 1 butternut squash
- 1 tbsp fresh ginger

For Garnishing
- Roasted chickpeas
- Coconut milk
- Cilantro

Instructions
1) Preheat the oven to 400 ° F.
2) On a parchment-lined baking sheet, place the carrots, butternut squash, and sliced shallots.
3) Splash with avocado oil & season with salt and pepper.
4) Toss lightly to coat.
5) Roast carrots and squash for 30 min, or until fork-tender.
6) Transfer to a blender with vegetable stock, coconut milk, ginger, salt, and pepper after cooling it somewhat. If you have a smaller blender, you may need to do it in two batches.
7) Blend until smooth and creamy, adding more stock or water if necessary to thin.
8) Garnish with roasted chickpeas, fresh cilantro, and a drizzle of coconut milk.

3.31 Chickpea and Vegetable Coconut Curry

Ready in 30 min
Servings: 4
Difficulty: Easy
Ingredients
- 1 tbsp virgin olive oil
- Steamed rice
- 1 red onion
- 3 garlic cloves
- 2 teaspoons of chili powder
- ¼ cup chopped cilantro
- 1 red bell pepper
- 1 tbsp ginger
- 4 scallions
- 1 small cauliflower

- 1 teaspoon coriander
- 3 tbsp red curry paste
- 14-ounce coconut milk
- 1 lime
- One can chickpeas
- 1½ cups of frozen peas
- Kosher salt & black pepper

Instructions
1) Heat the oil in a pan saucepan over medium heat. Cook, occasionally stirring, until the onion & bell pepper is almost cooked, approximately 5 minutes. Add the garlic and ginger and cook for 1 minute, or until fragrant.
2) Stir in the cauliflower & toss thoroughly. Cook, constantly stirring, until the chili powder, coriander, and red curry paste begins to caramelize, approximately 1 minute.
3) Add the coconut milk & bring the liquid to a low boil over medium heat. Cover the skillet and continue to cook for another 8 to 10 minutes until the cauliflower is soft.
4) Remove the cover and mix thoroughly to incorporate the lime juice and the curry. Return the mixture to a simmer; add salt and pepper, and add the chickpeas and peas.
5) If preferred, serve with rice. 1 tbsp cilantro & 1 tbsp scallions should be garnished on each serving.

3.32 Egg and Veggie Breakfast Bowl

Ready in 35 min
Servings: 4
Difficulty: Easy
Ingredients
- 1-pound sprouts
- 1-pound potatoes
- 1½ tbsp olive oil
- 2 cups of arugul

- 4 eggs
- 2 tbsp harissa
- 3 tbsp apple cider vinegar

Instructions

1) Preheat oven to 400 ° ° F. Using parchment paper, line a baking sheet.
2) Remove the Brussels sprouts from their stalks and cut them in half. Cut the sweet potatoes into cubes.
3) Place the brussels sprouts & sweet potatoes on a baking pan and spread them out evenly. Season with salt after drizzling the olive oil equally over veggies.
4) Roast for 17 to 20 minutes, until it's golden brown and soft.
5) Combine the harissa, olive oil, and cider vinegar in a small bowl.
6) Cook the eggs in a poaching or frying pan. (Need some assistance? Here's how to poach something, and here's how to fried something.)
7) To serve, split the brussels sprouts & sweet potatoes amongst four dishes and top with 12 cup arugula and 1 egg in each. 2 tbsp of harissa vinaigrette drizzled over each bowl

3.33 Apple Slaw & Kale Broccoli

Ready in 25 min
Servings: 6
Difficulty: Easy
Ingredients
- 1/2 cup cranberries
- 1-2 granny apples
- 2-3 tbsp goat cheese
- 2 bunches of kale
- 2 cups of shredded broccoli
- 1/2 cup of sunflower seeds
- 1/2 cup of slivered almonds
- 1 avocado peeled

Instructions

1) Mix all of the ingredients in a serving dish.

2) Toss with a vinaigrette made with Orange Muscat Champagne.

3.34 Champagne Vinaigrette with Orange Muscat

Ready in 25 min
Servings: 4
Difficulty: Easy
Ingredients
- 1 teaspoon Pure Maple Syrup
- 1 teaspoon Dijon Mustard
- Sprinkle of sea salt and pepper
- Lime juice
- 4 teaspoon Olive Oil
- 2 teaspoon Champagne Vinegar

Instructions

1) Mix all components in a glass jar
2) Place the lid on the jar and jiggle vigorously
3) Drizzle dressing over salad

3.35 Salmon with a Walnut-Rosemary Crusted

Ready in 20 min
Servings: 4
Difficulty: Easy
Ingredients
- 3 tbsp chopped walnuts
- 1 teaspoon extra-virgin olive oil
- 1 skinless salmon fillet
- Olive oil cooking spray
- Chopped parsley & lemon wedges
- 1 teaspoon of lemon juice
- 1 teaspoon of chopped rosemary
- ½ teaspoon of honey
- ½ teaspoon of salt
- ¼ teaspoon red pepper
- 3 tbsp breadcrumbs
- 2 teaspoons of Dijon mustard
- 1 clove garlic
- ¼ teaspoon of lemon zest

Instructions

1) Heat the oven to 425 ° F. Using parchment paper, line a large covered baking sheet.
2) In a small mixing bowl, lemon zest, mix mustard, garlic, lemon juice, rosemary, salt, honey, and crushed red pepper. In a separate small bowl, combine the panko, walnuts, and oil.
3) Place the fish on the baking sheet that has been prepared. Apply the mustard mixture to the fish and then top with panko mixture, pushing it in to adhere. Coat lightly with cooking spray.
4) Bake for 8 to 12 mins, depending on thickness, till its fish flakes easily with only a fork.
5) Garnish with parsley and, if preferred, serve with lemon wedges.

3.36 Latte with Matcha Green Tea

Ready in 10 min
Servings: 1
Difficulty: Easy
Ingredients
- 1 cup milk, low-fat
- 1 teaspoon of honey
- ¼ cup of boiling water
- 1 teaspoon powder of matcha tea

Instructions

1) In a blender, combine hot water and matcha powder until frothy. Bring the milk and honey to a near-boiling temperature. Whisk the milk vigorously until it becomes foamy. Fill a cup halfway with milk, then halfway with tea.

3.37 Spicy Cranberry Relish on Roasted Salmon

Ready in 30 min
Servings: 8
Difficulty: Easy
Ingredients

- 1 peeled Granny Smith apple
- 1 finely diced stalk celery
- 1 shallot
- 1 seeded serrano pepper
- 1 tbsp of balsamic vinegar
- 1 ½ teaspoon of salt
- ½ teaspoon of cracked black peppercorns
- 1 lemon zest
- 2 cups of frozen cranberries
- 2 tbsp of extra-virgin olive oil
- 2 teaspoons of Dijon mustard
- 2 ½ pounds of skin-on salmon fillet

Instructions

1) Preheat the oven to 400 ° F. Using parchment paper, line a wide baking sheet.
2) Arrange the salmon on the pan that has been prepared. With a fork or a pestle and mortar, mash the garlic, One teaspoon salt, peppercorns, and lemon zest into a pulp. 1 tbsp of oil & mustard should be added to a small bowl. Apply to the salmon. Bake for 15 minutes or until the meat flakes readily with a fork.
3) Meanwhile, in a food processor, finely chop the cranberries, shallot, and serrano. Add the apple, celery, vinegar, 1 tbsp parsley, the remaining 1 tbsp oil, and 1/2 teaspoon salt to a medium mixing bowl.
4) Toss the leftover 1 tbsp of parsley on top of the salmon & garnish with the relish & lemon wedges.

3.38 Lentil Soup

Ready in 40 min
Servings: 6
Difficulty: Easy
Ingredients
- 1 cup of turnip, chopped
- 3 radishes
- ¼ cup parsley leaves
- 1 tbsp fresh thyme, chopped

- 6 cups vegetable broth
- 2 tbsp extra-virgin olive oil
- 1 cup onion, chopped
- 1 cup of carrots, chopped
- 2 cups of brown lentils
- 5 cups of spinach
- 1 ½ tbsp balsamic vinegar
- ¾ teaspoon of salt

Instructions

1) On a programmed pressure multicooker, choose the Sauté setting. Allow for preheating on the High-temperature setting. Heat 1 tbsp of oil in the cooker until it shimmers. Simmer, sometimes stirring, until the onion is soft, approximately 5 minutes. Add the onion, carrots, turnip, & thyme; cook, occasionally stirring, till the onion is cooked, approximately 5 minutes. Combine the broth, lentils, and salt in a mixing bowl.
2) Press the Cancel button. Cover the pot with the lid and secure it. The pressure release handle should be in the Sealing position. Choose the Manual/Pressure Cook option. Set the timer for 10 minutes on high pressure.
3) Before removing the lid from the cooker, gently switch the steam release lever to Venting and let the steam completely escape (the float valve will drop; this will take approximately 5 minutes). Combine the spinach and vinegar in a mixing bowl.
4) In a small bowl, toss the radishes & parsley with the other 1 tbsp oil. Distribute the soup into 6 dishes and sprinkle with the radish combination.

3.39 Pecans with Spices

Ready in 1 hr 40 min
Servings: 20
Difficulty: Easy

Ingredients
- ½ teaspoon of salt
- ¼ teaspoon allspice
- ¼ teaspoon cloves
- 1 tbsp water
- 6 tbsp sugar
- Pinch of pepper
- 4 cups of pecan halves
- ¼ teaspoon of nutmeg
- Pinch of cinnamon

Instructions

1) Preheat the oven to 275 ° F. Using parchment paper, prepare a rimmed baking sheet.
2) In a large mixing bowl, whisk together the egg white, sugar, salt, water, allspice, cloves, cinnamon, nutmeg, and cayenne. Stir in the pecans until they are uniformly coated. On the prepared pan, distribute in a single layer.
3) Preheat oven to 350°F and bake for 30 mins. Bake for another 30 minutes, rotating the dish from back to front, till the nuts are crunchy & dry to the touch. Allow 20 minutes for the pan to cool fully. Before serving, separate the pieces.

3.40 Curry Soup with Roasted Cauliflower and Potatoes

Ready in 1 hr 30 min
Servings: 8
Difficulty: Easy
Ingredients
- 2 teaspoons of lime zest
- 2 tbsp lime juice
- 3 cups peeled russet potatoes
- 3 cups peeled sweet potatoes
- 1 can coconut milk
- 1 ½ teaspoon of grated ginger
- 1 fresh red chili pepper
- Chopped cilantro
- 3 cloves garlic
- 1 can tomato sauce
- ¾ teaspoon pepper

- ⅛ teaspoon cayenne pepper
- 4 cups vegetable broth
- 1 ¼ teaspoons of salt
- 1 small cauliflower
- 2 tbsp virgin olive oil
- 2 teaspoons of ground coriander
- 2 teaspoons of ground cumin
- 1 ½ teaspoon of ground cinnamon
- 1 chopped onion
- 1 cup of carrot
- 1 ½ teaspoon of ground turmeric

Instructions

1) Preheat the oven to 450 ° F.
2) In a small bowl, mix coriander, turmeric, cumin, cinnamon, salt, pepper, and cayenne. In a large mixing basin, combine the cauliflower with 1 tbsp of the oil, then add two tbsp of mixture & toss again. On a baking tray, spread inside a single layer. Then Roast cauliflower for 15 to 20 minutes, or even the edges are browned. Remove from the equation.
3) Meanwhile, in a large saucepan over medium-high heat, heat and cook 1 tbsp oil. Cook, often turning, until the onion and carrot begin to brown, 4 minutes. Reduce heat to low and cook, often turning, for 3 to 4 minutes, until the onions are tender. Combine the garlic, ginger, chili, and the remaining spice combination in a mixing bowl. Cook for another minute, stirring constantly.
4) Boil for 1 minute after adding the tomato sauce and scraping off any browned pieces. Combine the broth, potatoes, lime zest, sweet potatoes, and juice in a large mixing bowl. Bring to a boil, covered, over high heat. Reduce the heat to maintain a moderate simmer and cook, partly covered and stirring periodically, for 35 to 40 minutes, or until the veggies are soft.
5) Combine the coconut milk and roasted cauliflower in a mixing bowl. Return to low heat to finish heating.

3.41 Smoothie Bowl with Berries and Almonds

Ready in 10 min
Servings: 1
Difficulty: Easy

Ingredients
- ½ cup plain almond milk
- 5 tbsp sliced almonds
- ¼ teaspoon of ground cinnamon
- ⅔ cup raspberries
- ⅛ teaspoon of vanilla extract
- ¼ cup blueberries
- ½ cup banana
- ⅛ teaspoon of ground cardamom
- 1 tbsp coconut flakes

Instructions

1) In a blender, puree the banana, raspberries, almond milk, 3 tbsp almonds, cardamom, cinnamon, and vanilla until smooth.
2) Toss the blueberries, remaining 2 tbsp of almonds, and coconut into a bowl with the smoothie.

3.42 Chamomile Herbal Health Tonic

Ready in 20 min
Servings: 4
Difficulty: Easy
Ingredients
- 2 teaspoons ginger
- 4 slices of lemon
- 4 cups of boiling water
- 6 bags of chamomile tea
- 2 sprigs of rosemary
- 2-4 teaspoons honey
Instructions

1) In a large heatproof dish, combine honey, boiling water, ginger, tea bags, lemon, and rosemary.

2) Steep for 20 mins, stirring once in a while. Using a fine-mesh strainer, strain the liquid, pushing just on tea bags to extract as much liquid as possible.

3.43 Salmon with Miso and Maple

Ready in 15 min
Servings: 8
Difficulty: Easy
Ingredients
- ¼ cup of white miso
- 2 lemons
- 2 limes
- 1 skin-on salmon fillet
- Sliced scallions
- ¼ teaspoon of ground pepper
- Pinch of cayenne pepper
- 2 tbsp extra-virgin olive oil
- 2 tbsp maple syrup

Instructions
1) Preheat the broiler to high and place the rack in the top third of the oven. Using foil, line a large covered baking sheet.
2) Juice In a small dish, combines 1 lemon & 1 lime. Miso, maple syrup, pepper, oil, and cayenne pepper are whisked together. Pour the miso mixture on top of the salmon, skin-side down, in the prepared pan. Cut the leftover lemon and lime in halves and place cut-sides up around the fish.
3) Broil the salmon for 12 minutes or until it flakes easily with a fork. Served with lemon and orange halves on top, and scallions on the side, if preferred.

3.44 Green Smoothie Bowl with Almonds and Matcha

Ready in 10 min
Servings: 1
Difficulty: Easy

Ingredients
- ½ cup sliced banana
- ½ cup almond milk
- 5 tbsp slivered almonds
- ½ cup peaches
- 1 teaspoon maple syrup
- ½ ripe kiwi
- 1 cup spinach
- 1 ½ teaspoon matcha tea powder

Instructions
1) In a blender, puree almond milk, peaches, the banana, 3 tbsp almonds, matcha, spinach, and maple syrup until smooth.
2) Transfer the smoothie to a bowl and top with the leftover 2 tbsp slivered almonds and kiwi.

3.45 Bagna Cauda with Salmon and Fall Vegetables

Ready in 40 min
Servings: 4
Difficulty: Easy
Ingredients
- 1-pound potatoes, and sweet potato and cut into 1/2-inch-thick wedges
- 1 bunch trimmed broccolini
- 1 tablespoon virgin olive oil
- ½ teaspoon salt
- 1 pound salmon
- 2 medium heads of Belgian endive and leaves separated
- ½ small head of radicchio and cut into 1/2-inch-thick wedges

Bagna Cauda
- ⅓ cup virgin oil
- 2 tbsp vinegar
- 1 tbsp butter
- 2 cloves of garlic
- 8 fillets, anchovy

Instructions

1) Preheat the oven to 425 ° F. Using cooking spray, cover a large rimmed baking tray.
2) In a large mixing bowl, combine the potatoes & broccolini with 1 tbsp oil and 1/4 teaspoon salt. Place the potatoes on the baking sheet that has been prepared. Roast the potatoes for 15 minutes, turning halfway through.
3) Press the potatoes to a baking sheets edge. Season the salmon with the extra 1/4 teaspoon salt and place it in the center of the pan. Arrange the broccolini in a circular pattern around the fish. Roast for 6 to 10 minutes, or until the veggies are tender, as well as salmon, is just done through.
4) In the meanwhile, make the bagna cauda: In a small saucepan, heat the oil and garlic over medium-low heat till the garlic is aromatic, approximately 2 minutes. Lightly smash the anchovies until they break apart. Cook, often stirring, for another 2 mins over very low heat with vinegar and butter.
5) Arrange the salmon, potatoes, and broccolini on a plate with the fennel, endive, and radicchio. If desired, garnish with the saved fennel fronds. For dipping or drizzling, serve with bagna cauda.

3.46 Green Salad with Beets and Edamame

Ready in 15 min
Servings: 1
Difficulty: Easy
Ingredients
- ½ medium raw beet
- 1 tbsp plus 1 1/2 teaspoons vinegar
- 2 teaspoons olive oil
- Ground pepper to taste
- 2 cups salad greens, mixed

- 1 cup of shelled edamame
- 1 tbsp cilantro, chopped

Instructions

1) On a big dish, arrange the greens, edamame, and beet. In a small bowl, combine the vinegar, cilantro, oil, salt, and pepper. Drizzle the dressing over the salad & serve.

3.47 Salad of Purple Fruits

Ready in 15 min
Servings: 8
Difficulty: Easy
Ingredients
- 2 cups plums
- 2 cups of seedless black grapes
- 1 cup of Lime Yogurt for Fruit Salad Dressing
- 2 cups of halved blueberries
- 2 tbsp chopped basil, purple

Instructions

1) In a large mixing bowl, mix grapes, blueberries, plums, and basil. If preferred, serve with a yogurt dressing.

3.48 Cup of Noodles in Miso Soup with Shrimp and Green Tea Soba

Ready in 25 min
Servings: 3
Difficulty: Easy
Ingredients
- 3 cups of hot water
- 3 teaspoons of rice vinegar, unseasoned
- 1 ½ cups of sliced snow peas
- 9 ounces shrimp, peeled and cooked
- 4 tbsp of white miso
- 6 teaspoons of mirin
- 3 tbsp scallions, thinly sliced

- 1 dried kombu
- 1 ½ teaspoons wakame, dried
- 1 1/2 cups green tea soba noodles, dried

Instructions

1) In three 1 1/2-pint canning jars, combine 1 tablespoon & 1 teaspoon miso, 1 teaspoon vinegar, and 2 teaspoon mirin. Each jar should include 3 ounces shrimp, 1/2 cup snow peas, 1/2 teaspoon wakame, and 1/2 cup noodles. 1 tablespoon scallions on top of each. Place piece of kombu between the components & the jar's side. Put it in the fridge for three days if covered.

2) To prepare each jar, follow these steps: To dissolve the miso, add 1 cup of extremely hot water to the container, cover, and shake vigorously. Uncover and microwave for 2 to 3 minutes on High, in 1-minute increments, until boiling. Remove the kombu and throw it away. To ensure the miso is completely dissolved, give it a good stir. Allow resting for a few mins before serving.

3.49 Avocado Chickpea Salad Sandwich with Lemon and Cranberries

Ready in 10 min
Servings: 2
Difficulty: Easy
Ingredients

- 15 oz drained and rinsed chickpeas
- 2 tsp squeezed lemon fresh juice
- 1 ripe avocado
- 1/4 cup of dried cranberries
- 4 slices of whole grain bread
- Fresh salt & pepper for taste
- Toppings: Red onion, Arugula or spinach

Instructions

1) Mix chickpeas with a fork in a medium pan. Add in the avocado and crush it with a fork until it is smooth but still has some chunky pieces.

2) Combine the cranberries and lemon juice in a mixing bowl. To taste, season with salt & pepper. Keep refrigerated until ready to use.

3) Toast the bread and put 1/2 of the chickpea avocado salad on one piece when ready to serve. If preferred, garnish with arugula, red onion, or spinach. Top with the second toasted slice, then cut in halfway and enjoy.

3.50 Wild Rice and Buddha Bowl with Avocado, Kale and Orange

Ready in 40 min
Servings: 2
Difficulty: Easy

Ingredients

- 1 cup of wild rice
- 1 minced garlic clove
- 3 cups of water or vegetable broth
- 2 tbsp of rice vinegar
- 1 tbsp of chopped fresh mint
- 2 tbsp extra-virgin olive oil
- Salt & freshly black ground pepper

For dressing

- 1 roughly chopped of bunch kale
- 1 tsp of rice vinegar
- 2 tbsp of olive oil
- 1 orange and cut into segments
- ¼ cup of pomegranate seeds
- ¼ cup of pumpkin seeds
- 2 hard-boiled eggs
- ½ sliced avocado
- Salt & freshly black ground pepper

Instructions

1) Start making the rice, mix the rice, broth (or water, if using), and garlic in a medium saucepan. Over medium-high heat, bring the liquid to a simmer.
2) Reduce heat to low and continue to cook until the rice is cooked and all of the liquid has been evaporated, about 15 - 17 minutes.
3) Allow 5-10 minutes for the rice to cool before tossing it with the vinegar, olive oil, mint, salt & pepper.
4) Toppings: Toss kale with vinegar and olive oil in a medium bowl. Divide the rice into two dishes and top with kale in equal quantities.
5) Add 2 tbsp pomegranate seeds, half of the orange slices, half of avocado slices, 2 tsp pumpkin seeds, and then a hard-boiled egg to each of the bowls. Using salt & pepper, season the egg. Serve right away.

3.51 Chickpea & Vegetable Coconut Curry

Ready in 30 min
Servings: 2
Difficulty: Easy
Ingredients
- 1 tbsp olive oil extra-virgin
- 1 thinly sliced, red pepper
- 3 minced garlic cloves
- 1 thinly sliced red onion
- 1 tbsp minced fresh ginger
- 2 tbsp chili powder
- 1 cauliflower small, cut into small pieces
- 1 tsp ground coriander
- 3 tbsp paste of red curry
- 1 halved lime
- One 14-ounce coconut milk
- 1½ cups peas
- Salt & freshly black pepper
- Steamed rice (optional) for serving
- ¼ cup fresh cilantro chopped
- 4 thinly sliced scallions

Instructions

1) Heat the olive oil in a big saucepan over medium heat. Cook, occasionally stirring, until the onion & bell pepper is almost tender, approximately 5 minutes. Add the garlic and ginger and cook for 1 minute, or until fragrant.
2) Mix in the cauliflower until everything is nicely combined. Cook, constantly stirring, until the chili powder, coriander, and red curry paste begins to caramelize about 1 minute.
3) Over medium-low heat, add in the coconut milk & bring the mixture to a simmer. Cover the skillet and continue to cook for another 8 to 10 minutes, or when the cauliflower is soft.
4) Remove the cover and mix in the lime juice until everything is properly combined. Return the mixture to a simmer, season with pepper and salt, and add the chickpeas and peas.
5) If preferred, serve with rice. 1 tbsp scallions and 1 tbsp cilantro should be garnished on each serving.

3.52 White Turkey with Avocado

Ready in 20 min
Servings: 8
Difficulty: Easy
Ingredients

- 2 tbsp olive oil extra-virgin
- 1 diced onion
- 1 pound ground turkey
- 4 minced garlic cloves
- Salt & black pepper
- 1 tsp cayenne pepper
- 2 tsp of ground cumin
- 1 tsp of ground coriander
- 4 cups broth chicken
- One 15-ounce can of corn kernels, white beans
- 1 diced avocado

Instructions

1) Heat the olive oil in a big saucepan over medium heat. Add onion and cook for 6 to 8 minutes, or until transparent. Cook for another minute, or until the garlic is aromatic.
2) Cook for 5 to 7 minutes, or until the turkey is browned and thoroughly cooked. Season with salt & pepper, then add the cumin, coriander, and cayenne, and simmer for 1 to 2 minutes, until fragrant.
3) Add the broth and combine well. Over medium heat, bring the soup to a simmer. Reduce heat to low and cook for 30 to 35 minutes, or until a nice flavor emerges.
4) Boil for 2 to 3 minutes after adding the corn and beans.
5) Ladle the chili into bowls & top with 1-2 tbsp avocado to serve.
6) Serve right away.

Chapter 4: Dinner Recipes

4.1 Chicken & Snap Pea Stir-Fry

Ready in 20 min
Servings: 4
Difficulty: Easy
Ingredients

- 2 tbsp vegetable oil
- 2 tbsp Sriracha (optional)
- 1 bunch of thinly sliced scallions
- 2 cloves of minced garlic
- 1 thinly sliced red bell pepper
- 2 tbsp sesame seeds, plus more for finishing
- 2½ cups snap peas
- 1¼ cups thinly sliced boneless skinless chicken breast
- Freshly ground black pepper and Salt
- 2 tbsp rice vinegar
- 3 tbsp soy sauce or tamari
- 3 tbsp chopped fresh cilantro, plus more for finishing

Instructions

1) Heat the oil in a pan saute pan over medium heat. Saute the green onion and garlic for 1 minute or until aromatic. Saute the snap peas & the bell pepper for 2 to 3 minutes, or until just tender.
2) Add chicken and cook for 4 to 5 minutes, or until browned and thoroughly cooked, and even the veggies are soft.
3) Toss together the rice vinegar, soy sauce, Sriracha (if using), and sesame seeds. Allow 1 to 2 minutes for the mixture to boil.
4) Mix inside the cilantro, and then top with a sprinkling of sesame seeds and more cilantro. Serve right away.

4.2 Greek Turkey Burgers alongside Tzatziki Sauce

Ready in 1 hr 10 min
Servings: 4
Difficulty: Easy

Ingredients
Turkey Burgers

- 1 tbsp extra-virgin olive oil
- 1 egg
- 1 minced sweet onion
- ½ cup fresh parsley chopped
- 1 pound ground turkey
- ½ teaspoon of oregano
- ¼ teaspoon of red pepper flakes
- ¾ cup of bread crumbs
- 2 minced garlic cloves
- Freshly ground black pepper & salt

Tzatziki Sauce

- ½ diced European cucumber
- 1 tbsp extra-virgin olive oil
- 2 tbsp lemon juice
- 1 pinch garlic powder
- 1 cup Greek yogurt
- Freshly ground black pepper & salt
- ¼ cup fresh parsley, chopped

Burger Toppings

- ½ sliced red onion
- 4 hamburger buns, whole-wheat
- 2 sliced tomatoes
- 8 Boston lettuce leaves

Instructions

1) **To Make Turkey Burgers:** Heat oil in a small pan over medium heat. Cook for 3 to 4 minutes, or until the onion is soft. 1 minute later, add the garlic and cook until fragrant. Allow solidifying at room temperature before serving.

2) Combine the cooled onion mixture, egg, herbs, oregano, red pepper flakes, and ground turkey in a medium mixing dish. Mix in the bread crumbs, seasoning with salt and pepper as needed.

3) Preheat oven to 375 degrees Fahrenheit. Assemble the meat mixture into four equal-sized patties. Spray a big oven-safe skillet using nonstick cooking spray and heat it over medium-high heat.

4) In a pan, saute the patties from each side until nicely browned, about 4 to 5 minutes on each side. Transfer the pan to the oven and cook for another 15 to 17 minutes, or when the burgers are thoroughly cooked through.

5) **To Make Tzatziki Sauce:** Combine the yogurt, cucumber, olive oil, lime juice, and garlic powder in a medium mixing bowl. Season to taste using salt and pepper, and then add the parsley.

6) **Assemble the toppings:** Arrange all burgers on bottom half of a bun, top with approximately a quarter cup of tzatziki, 2 lettuce leaves, 2 tomato slices, & the top half of the bread. Serve right away.

4.3 Easy One-Pan Ratatouille

Ready in 1 hr 30 min
Servings: 4
Difficulty: Easy
Ingredients

- 2 tbsp thyme leaves
- 5 tbsp olive oil
- 2 sprigs oregano
- 1 thickly sliced small eggplant
- 1 thickly sliced medium red onion
- 2 smashed garlic cloves
- 2 thickly sliced medium summer squash
- 2 thickly sliced medium zucchini
- 3 thickly sliced medium tomatoes
- Freshly ground black pepper & Salt
- 2 halved small red bell peppers

- 1 cup tomato sauce

Instructions

1) Preheat oven to 375 degrees Fahrenheit. On a baking sheet, set four individual baking pans or one 9-inch rectangular baking dish.

2) Heat the oil and garlic in a small saucepan over medium-low heat. Cook for 1 minute or until aromatic. Remove the saucepan from the heat and soak the oregano for 15 minutes. Garlic and oregano should be removed and discarded.

3) Put 2 teaspoons olive oil into each tiny baking dish's base (or 2 tbsp on the base of the larger baking dish).

4) In the bottom of each baking dish, place 2 tbsp tomato puree (or 14 cups in the bigger baking dish).

5) In the prepared baking plates, arrange the onion, eggplant, summer squash, pepper, zucchini and tomato. Don't stress about being flawless or matching the slices; just make sure they're all packed in securely.

6) Drizzle the remaining oil equally over the top, and then apply the remaining tomato sauce on top. Season with salt & pepper and a sprig of thyme.

7) Roast for 25 to 30 minutes, or until soft and starting to brown on the top and edges. Allow five to ten minutes to cool before serving.

4.4 Hula Ginger vinaigrette with Seared Ahi Tuna Poke Salad & Wonton Crisps

Ready in 25 min Servings: 4 **Difficulty:** asy

Ingredients
Seared Ahi Tuna Poke

- 1/4 cup honey
- 1/4 cup of soy sauce

- 2 ahi tuna steaks
- 2 tbsp white and black sesame seeds toasted
- 1 teaspoon corn starch
- 1 teaspoon of chili garlic sauce
- 1/4 cup pineapple juice
- 20 square wonton wrappers cut into strips (to make this gluten-free, use corn tortillas)

Salad

- 1/2 cup fresh cilantro
- 1 cup fresh pineapple diced
- 1 sliced avocado
- 1 jalapeno or red chili sliced
- 4-8 cup spring greens

Hula Ginger Vinaigrette

- 1/2 cup toasted sesame oil or hot chili sesame oil
- 2 tbsp pineapple juice
- 2 tbsp rice vinegar
- 1/4 cup of soy sauce
- 1 teaspoon of chili garlic sauce or more to taste
- 1 lime zested & juiced
- 2 teaspoon grated fresh ginger
- 1 clove garlic minced or grated
- 1 tbsp tahini
- black and white sesame seeds toasted

Instructions

1) Bake oven at 400 degrees Fahrenheit.
2) Organize the wonton strips on an oiled baking sheet in such a thin layer (or as well you can arrange them). Using a spray of olive oil and then a generous amount of sea salt, coat the wontons. Bake for 5-10 minutes in a preheated oven, keeping an eye on them to ensure they don't burn. When they're a light golden hue and crisp, they're done. Remove the baking sheet from the microwave and put it aside.

3) Whisk with 1/4 cup of soy sauce & 1 teaspoon cornstarch in a small sauce saucepan until smooth. 1 teaspoon of chili garlic sauce, 1/4 cup pineapple juice, 1/4 cup of honey. Bring the saucepan to a boil on the stovetop over medium heat. Reduce the heat to low and cook for 3-4 minutes, or until the sauce thickens enough to cover the slotted spoon. Turn off the heat.
4) Heat the sesame oil in a big cast iron pan over high heat. In a pan, brown the tuna steaks for 1-2 minutes before flipping and brushing the browned side with soy sauce mixture. Take the steaks out from the pan after another minute or two of searing and coating it with the leftover soy sauce mixture. Cut the slices into strips.
5) In a mixing bowl, mix the cilantro, spring greens, avocado, pineapple chunks, and jalapeno (or red chili).
6) Make the vinaigrette in a separate small bowl. Mix the hot chili sesame oil, fresh ginger and garlic, soy sauce, pineapple juice, tahini, rice vinegar, chili garlic sauce, 1 teaspoon lime zest and juice, 1-2 teaspoons sesame seeds, black and white.
7) Arrange the greens on individual plates. Tuna, avocado slices, and wonton chips go on top. Drizzle the vinaigrette over the salad. Get your hands dirty!

4.5 Chicken marinated in Balsamic Vinegar, Brussels sprouts, Cranberries, and Pumpkin Seeds

Ready in 20 min
Servings: 4
Difficulty: Easy

Ingredients

- about 15 to 20 trimmed and halved lengthwise Brussels sprouts

- about 1 1/4 pounds diced into bite-sized pieces boneless skinless chicken breast
- 1 peeled and diced small-large shallot
- 3 tbsp olive oil
- for seasoning to taste, salt and pepper
- 1/2 cup sun-dried tomatoes (not oil-packed)
- 1/2 cup dried cranberries
- 1/4 cup balsamic vinegar
- 1/2 cup pumpkin seeds candied or roasted
- 2 tbsp honey

Instructions

1) Heat 2 tbsp of olive oil in a large pan over medium-high heat, then add Brussels sprouts cut side down and cook for 5 minutes until it's seared and softly golden brown.
2) Flip the sprouts and place them on one side of the grill. If you have to stack these on top of one another, that's ok.
3) Add the remaining 1 tbsp of olive oil (if required, add more) to the uncovered side of the plate and add the chicken, shallots, salt and pepper to taste, and cook for 4 to 5 minutes, or until chicken is 80 to 90% cooked through; toss and turn the chicken regularly.
4) Pour the balsamic vinegar and honey evenly over the top and whisk to mix.
5) Lower the heat to medium-low and continue to cook for 2 to 3 minutes, or until the meat is cooked through and the sprouts are crisp-tender.
6) Toss in the sun-dried tomatoes, cranberries, and pumpkin seeds, and mix well. Serve right away. The dish is best served warm and fresh, but it may be stored in an airtight container in the refrigerator for up to five days or frozen for up to three months.

4.6 Pineapple Fried Rice

Ready in 30 min
Servings: 4
Difficulty: Easy
Ingredients

- 3 cups cooked brown rice
- 1/2 cup frozen peas
- 2 cups pineapple diced
- 1/2 cup diced ham
- 1/4 teaspoon white pepper
- 2 green sliced onions
- 3 tbsp soy sauce
- 1 tbsp sesame oil
- 1/2 teaspoon ginger powder
- 2 tbsp olive oil
- 2 cloves garlic, minced
- 1 diced onion
- 2 peeled and grated carrots
- 1/2 cup frozen corn

Instructions

1) Combine sesame oil, soy sauce, ginger powder, and white pepper in a small bowl; leave aside.
2) In a large frying pan or wok, heat the olive oil on medium-high heat. Add the onion and ginger to the skillet and cook, often stirring, for 3-4 minutes, or until onions are translucent. Stir in the carrots, corn, peas, and simmer, frequently stirring, for 3-4 minutes, or until the veggies are soft.
3) Combine the pineapple, ham, rice, green onions, and soy sauce combination in a large mixing bowl. Cook, stirring continually, for approximately 2 minutes, or until well cooked.
4) Serve right away.

4.7 Baked Sesame-Ginger Salmon in Parchment

Ready in 30 min
Servings: 4
Difficulty: Easy
Ingredients

- 1 teaspoon sesame oil
- 2 tbsp honey
- 2 tbsp soy sauce
- 2 tbsp grated fresh ginger
- Pinch of red pepper flakes
- 2 large zucchini, thinly sliced & halved lengthwise
- Four 6-ounce skinless salmon fillets
- 1 red onion, thinly sliced & halved
- 1 quartered lime
- 1 teaspoon garlic powder
- 4 teaspoons sesame seeds

Instructions

1) Preheat oven to 350 degrees Fahrenheit. Prepare four parchment sheets (around 15 by 17 inches). To produce a crease, wrap each piece in half, then unfold and put it aside.
2) Combine the sesame oil, soy sauce, garlic, ginger powder, honey, and red pepper flakes in a small bowl.
3) Assemble the parchment packs one by one. Put a quarter of zucchini in an equal layer on one side of a sheet of paper & top with the quarter of the red onion. Squeeze one lime segment over the veggies liberally.
4) Top the veggies with a salmon fillet. Brush the soy sauce mixture thoroughly over the fish and sprinkle with one teaspoon of sesame seeds.
5) To thoroughly seal the package, wrap the blank side of the paper over the fish and then wrap the two sides inward toward the fish, forming multiple creases.

6) Use the remaining paper and ingredients to repeat the process. Place the prepared packets on a baking tray and bake for 16 to 18 minutes, or until the salmon is thoroughly cooked.
7) To serve, either takes the fish and vegetables from the packet and place them on plates or cut holes in the top of the paper and serve the fish and vegetables in the paper. Serve right away.

4.8 Mediterranean roast chicken with turmeric & fennel

Ready in 1 hr
Servings: 4-6
Difficulty: Easy
Ingredients

- ½ cup extra virgin olive oil
- Salt and Pepper
- ½ cup dry white wine
- ½ cup orange juice
- 1 lime juice
- 2 tbsp yellow mustard
- 1 tbsp garlic powder
- ¾ tbsp ground turmeric spice
- 1 teaspoon ground coriander
- 1 large sliced into half-moons sweet onion
- 3 tbsp brown sugar
- 1 large sliced fennel bulb
- 6 pieces bone-in, skin-on chicken (chicken legs or breasts)
- 2 Oranges sliced unpeeled
- 1 thinly sliced lime
- 1 teaspoon sweet paprika

Instructions

1) Make the marinade first. Combine the first six ingredients in a large mixing bowl or deep dish: white wine, olive oil, orange juice, mustard, lime juice, and brown sugar.

2) Combine the spices in a small bowl: garlic powder, turmeric, paprika, coriander, salt & pepper. Half of the spice mix should now be added to the liquid marinade. To blend, stir everything together.
3) Press the fillets dry and season thoroughly with the remaining spice mixture. Peel the chicken wings slightly & rub part of the spice mixture beneath the skin.
4) Combine the marinated chicken and the other marinade ingredients in a large mixing dish. Incorporate the meat well into the marinade. Cover and marinate for 1-2 hours (skip the marination if you do not have time).
5) Preheat to 475 degrees F when ready. Transfer the chicken, including the marinade and the rest of the ingredients, to a large baking sheet and arrange everything in one layer. Make sure the skin of the bird is facing up. If desired, season with a pinch of salt and additional brown sugar.
6) Grill for 45 mins or until chicken is fully done and the skin has browned attractively. The internal temperature of the chicken must be 170 degrees F.

4.9 One-Pan Eggs with Tomatoes & Asparagus

Ready in 30 min
Servings: 4
Difficulty: Easy
Ingredients

- 1 pint cherry tomatoes
- 2 pounds asparagus
- 2 tbsp olive oil
- 4 eggs
- Salt and pepper
- 2 teaspoons chopped fresh thyme

1) Preheat oven to 400 ° degrees Fahrenheit. Using nonstick cooking spray, grease a baking sheet.
2) Organize the asparagus & cherry tomatoes on the baking tray in an equal layer. Pour the olive oil over veggies and season to taste with thyme, salt, and pepper.
3) Roast for 10 to 12 minutes, or until the asparagus is almost soft and the tomatoes are wrinkled.
4) Scatter the eggs over the asparagus and sprinkle with salt.
5) Bake for another 8 mins until the egg whites get set; however, the yolks are mostly jiggly.
6) Arrange the asparagus, tomatoes, and eggs on four dishes to serve.

4.10 Citrus Salad with Sweet Potato Bulgur

Ready in 1 hr
Servings: 6
Difficulty: Easy
Ingredients

- Black pepper for taste
- 1/2 cup finely chopped mint
- 1 cup finely chopped parsley
- 1/4 cup finely chopped red onion
- 2 tbsp orange zest
- 1 tbsp avocado oil
- 2 teaspoons maple syrup
- Coarse salt and black pepper
- 1/4 cup olive oil
- 1/4 cup freshly squeezed orange juice
- 1 tbsp red wine vinegar
- 1 small clove garlic
- 1/2 teaspoon salt
- 2 tbsp lemon juice
- 2 medium-sized sweet potatoes, peeled and cubed
- 1 1/4 cups bulgur wheat

Instructions

Instructions

1) Oven preheated to 425 degrees Fahrenheit. Combine the sweet potatoes, cooking oil, syrup, a big teaspoon of coarse salt, and a couple of grinds of pepper in a mixing bowl. Place the potatoes on a baking sheet coated with parchment paper and bake for 35-40 minutes until it's very soft and lightly caramelized, stirring halfway through.

2) Boil 3 1/2 cups water while the potatoes are roasting. Reduce the heat to a low and add the bulgur. Cook, stirring periodically, for 8 minutes. Take the bulgur off the heat, cover it, and set it aside for 10 minutes. Drain the bulgur and fluff it with a fork to remove any extra water.

3) Combine the olive oil, salt, orange juice, red wine vinegar, lemon juice, garlic, and pepper in a mixing bowl and whisk to combine.

4) When the potatoes are done, combine them in a large mixing dish with the cooked bulgur, mint, orange zest, parsley and red onion. Toss in the dressing. Toss everything together until fully combined, then taste and adjust spices as required. Serve the food.

4.11 Citrus Salad with Sweet Potato Bulgur

Ready in 30 min
Servings: 4
Difficulty: Easy
Ingredients

- 1 White Onion
- 3 Carrots
- 3 cloves minced garlic
- 1 inch finely grated Piece of Fresh Ginger
- 1 tbsp Lemon Juice

- 2 inch finely grated Piece of fresh Turmeric
- Black Sesame Seeds
- Canned Coconut Milk
- 4 cups (950ml) Vegetable Stock

Instructions

1) Thinly slice the ginger and turmeric, then chop the onion as well as carrot into tiny bits (no need to be perfect since everything will be mixed at the end).

2) In the bottommost of a deep stockpot, heat a little olive oil and saute onion for 3 minutes, or until transparent, next mix the minced turmeric, ginger and garlic, and cook for another minute.

3) Add the chopped carrots and continue to cook for the next 2 minutes. Now mix the veggie stock and boil for another 20-25 minutes, or until the carrots are tender and cooked through.

4) Mix the soup with a stick blender until smooth, or transfer to an upright blender and blend. Garnish with a splash of buttermilk and some black sesame seeds after adding the lemon juice.

4.12 Roasted Salmon in a Single Pan with Potatoes and Romaine

Ready in 40 min
Servings: 4
Difficulty: Easy
Ingredients

- 4 tbsp extra-virgin olive oil, divided
- 1 teaspoon lemon juice
- Kosher salt and freshly ground black pepper for taste
- 1 pound baby Yukon Gold potatoes
- 1 tbsp unsalted melted butter
- ¼ teaspoon paprika
- 2 hearts romaine lettuce
- Four 6-ounce salmon fillets

Instructions

1) Preheat oven to 400 ° degrees Fahrenheit.
2) Mix the potatoes with 2 tbsp olive oil in a medium mixing basin; spread out in a thin layer on a baking tray. 15 minutes in the oven, until the potatoes are slightly browned and fork-tender.
3) In the meantime, chop the romaine hearts in half and drizzle with 3 tbsp olive oil and lemon juice. Salt & pepper to taste. Remove from the equation.
4) Brush the melted butter over the salmon fillets using a pastry brush. Season each fillet to taste with paprika, salt, and pepper.
5) Set the romaine hearts, salmon, and potatoes on the baking sheet. Continue roasting for another 5 to 7 minutes or until the lettuce is soft and also the fish is done through. Divide the potatoes, romaine, and salmon across four dishes to serve.

4.13 Peppers stuffed with ground turkey and sweet potatoes

Ready in 1 hr
Servings: 4
Difficulty: Easy
Ingredients

- 1 tbsp virgin olive oil
- 2 cups of grass-fed turkey
- 2 cloves minced garlic
- ½ cup of homemade tomato sauce
- red pepper to taste
- salt and pepper
- 1⅔ cups of diced sweet potatoes
- 2 large bell peppers, cut in half
- feta cheese garnish
- ½ cup diced onions
- fresh parsley for garnish

Instructions

1) Preheat the oven to 350 degrees Fahrenheit.
2) Heat the olive oil in a pan over medium-high heat.
3) Stir in the garlic and ground turkey. Cook for approximately 10 minutes, until the chicken, is no longer pink, stirring periodically. As the meat cooks, be careful to split it up with a wooden spoon.
4) Stir in the onions and sauté until golden brown.
5) Put the sweet potatoes and simmer, covered, until they are soft. It takes roughly 8 minutes to complete.
6) Don't forget to stir now and again. Toss in the tomato sauce, crushed red pepper, salt, and freshly ground black pepper to taste. When cook the sweet potatoes, add extra olive oil or a splash of water if required.
7) Place the peppers in a prepared baking dish, cavity side up.
8) Stuff each half of bell pepper with both the chopped turkey-sweet potato mixture.
9) Bake for 30 mins, uncovered, and when the peppers are tender and cooked.
10) Remove the dish from the oven and top with feta cheese and parsley.

4.14 Quinoa Bowl with Mediterranean Chicken

Ready in 30 min
Servings: 4
Difficulty: Easy
Ingredients

- 1 pound trimmed boneless chicken breasts
- 2 tbsp of finely chopped parsley
- ¼ teaspoon of ground pepper
- 1 7-ounce jar of roasted red peppers
- ¼ cup of slivered almonds

- ¼ teaspoon of salt
- 4 tbsp of virgin olive oil
- 1 small crushed clove garlic
- ½ teaspoon of ground cumin
- ¼ teaspoon of crushed red pepper
- 2 cups cooked quinoa
- 1 teaspoon of paprika
- ¼ cup chopped of pitted Kalamata olives
- 1 cup of diced cucumber
- ¼ cup of crumbled feta cheese
- ¼ cup of finely chopped red onion

Instructions
1) Preheat the broiler to high and place a rack in the top third of the oven. Using foil, cover a rimmed baking sheet.
2) Season the chicken using salt and pepper before placing it on the baking sheet. Broil, rotating once, for 14 to 18 minutes, until an instant-read input signal in the thickest section registers 165 degrees F. Using a cutting board, shred or slice the chicken.
3) In a tiny food processor, combine the peppers, almonds, 2 tbsp oil, paprika, cumin, garlic, and red pepper. Puree until the mixture is pretty smooth.
4) In a medium mixing bowl, combine the quinoa, olives, red onion, and the remaining 2 tbsp oil.
5) To assemble, distribute the quinoa combination among four bowls and top evenly with cucumber, chicken, and red pepper sauce. Garnish with feta cheese and parsley.

4.15 Salad with Tomatoes, Cucumbers, and White Beans with Basil Vinaigrette

Ready in 25 min **Servings: 4 Difficulty** Easy
Ingredients
- ¼ cup of virgin olive oil
- ½ cup fresh basil leaves
- 3 tbsp of vinegar

- 1 tbsp of finely chopped shallot
- 1 teaspoon of honey
- ¼ teaspoon of salt
- 2 teaspoons of Dijon mustard
- ¼ teaspoon of ground pepper
- 1 (15 ounces) can rinse cannellini beans, low-sodium
- 10 cups mixed green salad
- 1 cup halved grape of tomatoes or cherry
- ½ cucumber, sliced & halved lengthwise

Instructions
1) In a tiny food processor, combine basil, vinegar, oil, shallot, honey mustard, salt, and pepper. Process until the mixture is largely smooth. Place in a large mixing basin. Combine the greens, beans, tomatoes, and cucumber in a large mixing bowl. Toss to coat evenly.

4.16 Smoky Chickpeas & Greens with Roasted Salmon

Ready in 40 min **Servings: 4 Difficulty:** asy
Ingredients
- ¼ teaspoon of garlic powder
- 2 tbsp of virgin olive oil
- ½ teaspoon of salt, divided, plus a pinch
- 1 tbsp of smoked paprika
- ⅓ cup of buttermilk
- ¼ cup of mayonnaise
- ¼ cup of chopped fresh chives & dill, and garnish
- ½ teaspoon of ground pepper, divided
- 10 cups of chopped kale

- 1 (15 ounces) can rinsed chickpeas
- 1 ¼ pounds of wild salmon, and cut into 4 portions
- ¼ cup of water

Instructions
1) Preheat oven to 425 degrees F, with racks in the top third and center.
2) In a medium mixing dish, mix 1 tablespoon oil, paprika, and 1/4 teaspoon salt. Toss the chickpeas with the paprika mixture after fully drying them. Place on a baking tray to cool. Bake the chickpeas for 30 minutes on the top rack, stirring twice.
3) Meanwhile, in a blender, mix the buttermilk, mayonnaise, herbs, 1/4 teaspoon pepper, and garlic powder until smooth. Remove from the equation.
4) In a large skillet, heat and cook 1 tablespoon of oil over medium heat. Cook, stirring periodically, for 2 minutes after adding the kale. Cook, occasionally stirring, until the kale is soft, approximately 5 minutes longer. Remove the pan from the heat and add a little salt.
5) Take the chickpeas out of the oven and place them on one side of the pan. Season, the salmon with the leftover 1/4 teaspoon salt and pepper on the opposite side. Bake for 5 to 8 minutes, or until salmon is just done through.
6) Pour the reserved dressing over the salmon and serve with the greens and chickpeas.

4.17 Pasta Salad with Pesto

Ready in 20 min
Servings: 5
Difficulty: Easy
Ingredients
- 1 cup small of broccoli florets
- 8 ounces 3 cups of whole-wheat fusilli
- ¼ cup of toasted pine nuts
- 2 tbsp of mayonnaise
- ¼ cup of grated Parmesan cheese
- 2 tbsp virgin olive oil
- 2 tbsp of lemon juice
- 1 large quartered clove garlic
- ¾ teaspoon of salt
- 1 cup quartered tomatoes
- 2 cups fresh basil leaves
- ½ teaspoon of ground pepper

Instructions
1) A big pot of water should be brought to a boil. Cook the fusilli according to the package guidelines. Stir in broccoli 1 min until the pasta is done. Cook for 1 min before draining and rinsing beneath cold water to end the cooking process.
2) In a little food processor, combine basil, Parmesan, oil, mayonnaise, lemon juice, garlic, pine nuts, salt, and pepper. Process until the mixture is practically smooth. Place in a large mixing basin. Toss in the pasta, broccoli, and tomatoes. Toss to coat evenly.

4.18 Roasted Greek Fish with Vegetables

Ready in 55 min
Servings: 4
Difficulty: Easy
Ingredients
- 5 coarsely chopped garlic cloves
- 1 pound fingerling potatoes
- 2 tbsp of olive oil
- ½ teaspoon of sea salt
- 4 5 to 6-ounce skinless salmon fillets
- 2 medium red, yellow & orange sweet peppers, cut into rings
- ½ teaspoon of ground black pepper
- 2 cups cherry tomatoes
- 1 lemon
- 1 ½ cups of chopped fresh parsley (1 bunch)
- 1 Tbsp crushed dried oregano
- ¼ cup of snipped fresh oregano
- ¼ cup pitted kalamata olives

Instructions

1) Heat the oven to 425 °. In a large mixing basin, place the potatoes. Toss with 1 tbsp oil, garlic, and 1/8 tsp. Salt & black pepper; stir to coat. Cover with foil and move to a 15x10-inch baking sheet. 30 minutes of roasting

2) In the meanwhile, defrost any frozen fish. Sweet peppers, parsley, olives, oregano, tomatoes and 1/8 teaspoon salt and black pepper all go into the same dish. Drizzle the leftover 1 tbsp oil over the top and toss to coat.

3) Rinse the fish and pat it dry. Add the remaining 1/4 teaspoon salt and black pepper to taste. Top potatoes with the sweet pepper mixture and fish. Roast for another 10 minutes, uncovered, or until fish flakes easily.

4) Lemon zest should be removed. Lemon juice should be squeezed over the fish and veggies. Add a dash of zest.

4.19 Mediterranean Stew in a Slow Cooker

Ready in 6 hrs 45 min **Servings:** 6
Difficulty: Easy

Ingredients

- 3 tablespoons of virgin olive oil
- Fresh basil leaves
- 6 lemon of wedges (Elective)
- ½ teaspoon of crushed red pepper
- ¼ teaspoon of ground pepper
- 1 (15 ounces) can rinse chickpeas (no-salt-added)
- 1 bunch lacinato kale, stemmed & chopped (around 8 cups)
- 1 tbsp of lemon juice
- 3 cups of low-sodium vegetable broth
- 1 cup of chopped onion
- ¾ cup of chopped carrot
- 4 minced of cloves garlic
- 1 teaspoon of dried oregano
- ¾ teaspoon of salt
- 2 (14 ounces) cans of fire-roasted diced tomatoes

Instructions

1) In a 4-quart slow cooker, add broth, onion, garlic, tomatoes, oregano, carrot, salt, red pepper, and pepper. Cook on low for six hours, covered.

2) Pour 1/4 cup of the slow cooker's cooking liquid into a small basin. Using a fork, mash 2 tablespoons of chickpeas until smooth.

3) In the slow cooker, combine the mashed chickpeas, lemon juice, greens and the remaining whole chickpeas. To blend, stir everything together. Cover and simmer on low for 30 minutes or until the kale is cooked.

4) Divide the stew into 6 bowls and sprinkle with oil. Serve with basil as a garnish. If desired, garnish with lemon slices.

4.20 Portobello Mushrooms with Greek Stuffing

Ready in 25 min
Servings: 4
Difficulty: Easy

Ingredients

- 3 tbsp virgin olive oil
- 1 minced clove garlic
- ¼ teaspoon of salt
- 1 cup of chopped spinach
- 1 tbsp of chopped fresh oregano
- ½ cup quartered tomatoes
- ⅓ cup of crumbled feta cheese
- 4 portobello mushrooms (about 14 ounces) stems, clean and gills removed
- 2 tbsp pitted & sliced Kalamata olives
- ½ teaspoon of ground pepper

Instructions

1) Preheat oven to 425 degrees Fahrenheit.

2) In a small bowl, mix 2 tbsp oil, garlic, 1/4 teaspoon pepper, and salt.

Apply the oil mixture all over the mushrooms using a silicone brush. Put on a large rimmed baking sheet for 8 to 10 minutes or when the mushrooms are largely tender.

3) In a medium mixing bowl, add feta, tomatoes, spinach, oregano and olives the outstanding 1 tbsp of oil. Remove the mushrooms from oven after they have softened & fill with spinach mixture. After that bake for approximately 10 minutes or when tomatoes have wilted.

4.21 Ravioli with Artichokes and Olives from the Mediterranean

Ready in 15 min
Servings: 4
Difficulty: Easy
Ingredients

- 2 (8 ounces) packages of frozen or refrigerated spinach & ricotta ravioli
- ¼ cup of sliced Kalamata olives
- ½ cup of drained oil-packed sun-dried tomatoes
- 1 (15 ounces) rinsed of cannellini beans
- 3 tbsp of toasted pine nuts
- 1 (10 ounces) thawed frozen quartered artichoke hearts
- ¼ cup of chopped basil

Instructions
1) A huge pot of water should be brought to a boil. Cook ravioli as directed on the box. Set aside after draining and tossing with 1 tbsp of the leftover oil.
2) Inside a large nonstick skillet, heat the remaining 1 tbsp oil over medium heat. Sauté for 2 to 3 mins, or until artichokes and beans are cooked through.
3) Toss the prepared ravioli, sun-dried tomatoes, pine nuts, olives and basil together in a large mixing bowl.

4.22 Provençal Baked Fish with Mushrooms and Roasted Potatoes

Ready in 1 hr
Servings: 4
Difficulty: Easy
Ingredients

- 1 pound of cubed red potatoes
- 2 tbsp of extra-virgin olive oil
- 1 pound of trimmed & sliced mushrooms
- ¼ teaspoon of ground pepper
- ¼ teaspoon of salt
- 2 peeled & sliced cloves garlic
- 14 ounces halibut and cut into 4 portions, grouper or cod fillet
- 4 tbsp of lemon juice
- Fresh thyme for garnish
- 1 teaspoon of herbs de Provence

Instructions
1) Turn the oven to 425 ° F.
2) In a large mixing bowl, combine potatoes, mushrooms, 1 tablespoon oil, salt, and pepper. Fill a 9x13-inch baking sheet halfway with the mixture. Roast for 30 to 40 minutes or until the veggies are barely tender.
3) Stir in the veggies, followed by the garlic. Arrange the fish on top. Drizzle with the leftover 1 tbsp. oil and lemon juice. Herbs de Provence should be sprinkled on top. Bake for 10 to 15 minutes, or until the salmon is translucent in the middle and flakes readily. If desired, garnish with thyme.

4.23 Mediterranean Chicken, Brussels sprouts, and Gnocchi on a Sheet Pan

Ready in 40 min **Servings:** 4 **Difficulty:** Easy
Ingredients

- 2 tbsp of chopped oregano
- 2 large cloves of garlic, minced

- 4 tbsp extra-virgin olive oil, divided
- 1 (16 ounces) package shelf-stable gnocchi
- ½ teaspoon of ground pepper
- 1 pound Brussels sprouts, quartered & trimmed
- 1 cup sliced of red onion
- 4 boneless, trimmed chicken thighs
- 1 tbsp of vinegar
- 1 cup of halved cherry tomatoes
- ¼ teaspoon of salt

- 3-pound squash spaghetti, lengthwise halved & seeded
- 8 ounces of sliced cremini mushrooms
- ½ cup julienned sun-dried tomatoes
- ½ teaspoon of salt
- 2 teaspoons of nutritional yeast
- 1 cup basil leaves fresh
- 2 cloves of coarsely chopped garlic
- 3 tbsp of lemon juice
- ½ teaspoon of ground pepper

Instructions

1) Heat the oven to 450 ° F.
2) In a large mixing bowl, combine 2 tbsp oil, 1 teaspoon oregano, half of the garlic, 1/4 teaspoon pepper, and 1/8 teaspoon salt. Toss in the Brussels sprouts, gnocchi, and onion to coat. Place on a broad-rimmed baking sheet and spread out evenly.
3) In a large mixing bowl, combine 1 tbsp oil, the remaining 1 tbsp oregano, the remaining garlic, the remaining 1/4 teaspoon pepper, and 1/8 teaspoon salt. Toss in the chicken to coat. Place the chicken in the vegetable mixture and tuck it in. 10 minutes of roasting
4) Remove the pan from the heat and mix in the tomatoes. Continue roasting for another 10 minutes or until the Brussels sprouts are soft and the chicken is only cooked through. In a mixing bowl, combine the vegetable combination, vinegar, and the other 1 tbsp oil.

4.24 Spaghetti Squash with Vegan Pesto, Mushrooms, and Sun-Dried Tomatoes

Ready in 30 min
Servings: 4
Difficulty: Easy
Ingredients
- ⅓ cup of unsalted raw cashews
- 4 tbsp extra-virgin olive oil, divided

Instructions

1) Cut-side down, place squash halves in an oven dish with 2 tbsp water. Microwave on High for 10 to 14 minutes, uncovered, until soft. (Alternatively, cut side down on a baking sheet and bake, put squash halves.) Preheat the oven to 400 degrees F and bake for 40 - 50 minutes, or until the potatoes are soft. You may also use a pressure cooker/multi-cooker to cook the squash.
2) In a large skillet, heat 1 tbsp oil over medium heat. Add the mushrooms, tomatoes, and 1/4 teaspoon salt; simmer, occasionally turning, for 5 to 6 minutes, or until the mushrooms are tender and beginning to brown. Remove the pan from the heat.
3) In a food processor, combine basil, an additional 3 tbsp oil, cashews, lemon juice,
Garlic, nutritional yeast, and the remaining 1/4 teaspoon salt and pepper. Process until the mixture is largely smooth.
4) Remove the squash flesh from the shell into a strainer with a fork. To eliminate some of the liquid, softly press on the skin. Squash should be divided among four plates. Place a scoop of basil pesto on top of each dish of the mushroom mixture.

4.25 Grilled Salmon with Vegetables

Ready in 25 min
Servings: 4
Difficulty: Easy
Ingredients

- 2 red, trimmed, halved and seeded yellow, orange bell peppers
- 1 tablespoon of extra virgin olive oil
- ½ teaspoon of salt
- 1 lemon, cut into 4 wedges
- ½ teaspoon of ground pepper
- 1 medium red onion and cut into 1-inch wedges
- 1 ¼ pounds salmon fillet and cut into 4 portions
- ¼ cup thinly sliced basil fresh
- 1 medium halved lengthwise zucchini

Instructions
1) Preheat the grill to medium-high.
2) Oil the zucchini, peppers, and onion, then season with 1/4 teaspoon salt. Season the salmon with the additional 1/4 teaspoon salt and pepper.
3) Place the veggies and salmon slices on the grill, skin-side down. Cook the veggies for 4 to 6 minutes on each side, stirring just once twice until barely cooked and grill marks form. Cook the salmon for 8 to 10 minutes, without turning it, till it flakes when checked with a fork.
4) Once the veggies have cooled enough to handle, coarsely chop them and combine them in a large mixing basin. If preferred, remove the skin of the salmon fillets and serve with the veggies. Serve with a lemon slice and 1 tablespoon basil on top of each plate.

4.26 Pizza with goat cheese

Ready in 30 min **Servings:** 2 **Difficulty:**Easy

Ingredients
- 1 (7 inches) crust of the whole wheat pizza
- 1 teaspoon of olive oil
- 1 sliced of Roma tomato
- 2 ounces cooked turkey breast
- 1 cup fresh baby spinach
- ¼ cup sliced red onion
- ¼ cup of crumbled goat cheese
- 2 tbsp of fresh snipped basil

Instructions
1) Using a pastry brush, coat the pizza dough with oil. Tomato, spinach, turkey, goat cheese & red onion go on top. Bake according to the instructions on the crust box.
2) Sprinkle with basil before serving.

4.27 Soup with Mediterranean Chicken and Chickpeas in a Slow Cooker

Ready in 4 hr 20 min
Servings: 6
Difficulty: Easy
Ingredients
- 4 cups of water
- 1 large finely chopped yellow onion
- 1 ½ cups dried chickpeas, soaked overnight
- 1 (15 ounces) fire roasted diced tomatoes

- 2 tbsp of tomato paste
- 4 cloves of chopped garlic
- 4 teaspoons of ground cumin
- ¼ teaspoon of cayenne pepper
- 1 bay leaf
- ¼ teaspoon of ground pepper
- 2 pounds trimmed chicken thighs & skin removed
- 4 teaspoons of paprika
- 1 (14 ounces) can drain & quarter artichoke hearts
- ¼ cup halved oil-cured olives
- ½ teaspoon of salt
- ¼ cup chopped fresh parsley or cilantro

Instructions

1) Place chickpeas in a 6-quart or bigger slow cooker, drained. Stir together 4 cups water, tomatoes onion, garlic, cumin bay leaf, cayenne, paprika, tomato paste and ground pepper. Toss in the chicken.
2) Cook on medium for eight hours or moderate for 4 hours, covered.
3) Allow the chicken to cool slightly on a clean chopping board. Bay leaf should be discarded. Stir together the artichokes, olives, and salt in the slow cooker. Remove the bones from the chicken and shred them. Add the chicken to the broth and mix well. Serve with parsley on top (or cilantro).

4.28 Pasta with Whole-Grain Sauce and Parmesan

Ready in 1 hr 55 min
Servings: 8
Difficulty: Easy
Ingredients
- 2 cloves of garlic
- ½ teaspoon of kosher salt
- ½ teaspoon of smoked paprika
- ¼ cup grated Parmesan cheese
- ½ of a (28 ounce) whole peeled plum tomatoes (1 1/3 cups)

- ½ cup of toasted whole almonds
- 3 tbsp of olive oil
- 2 tbsp of chopped fresh Italian parsley, add more for garnish
- 1 tbsp of sherry vinegar
- 12 ounces of whole-grain pasta
- 1 tbsp of honey
- 2 large red bell peppers

Instructions

1) Preheat the oven to 400 Fahrenheit. A baking sheet should be lightly oiled. Remove the stems, seeds, and membranes from bell peppers by cutting them in half lengthwise. Set the pepper slices, cut sides up upon the baking sheet that has been prepared. Roast for 45 minutes until the pepper is tender and the skins easily peel away. Wrap the peppers in plastic wrap and place them in a bowl. Allow for 30 minutes of cooling time or until cold enough to handle. The skins should be peeled off and discarded.
2) To make the sauce, in a blender or food processor, mix the roasted peppers, almonds, tomatoes, oil, 2 tbsp parsley, sherry vinegar, honey, garlic, salt, &smoky paprika. Blend or process until almost smooth, covered. (Because of the almonds, the sauce will have a coarse texture.)
3) Place the sauce in a medium pot and stir to combine. Bring to a boil, and then turn off the heat. Cook for 20 minutes.
4) Meanwhile, cook the pasta as directed on the box; drains. Pour sauce above the spaghetti and top with Parmesan cheese. Garnish with more parsley, if preferred.

4.29 Farfalle with Tuna, Fennel & Lemon

Ready in 30 min
Servings: 4
Difficulty: Easy
Ingredients
1) 2 tbsp of snipped fresh Italian parsley
2) 1 teaspoon of shredded lemon peel
3) 2 cloves of minced garlic
4) ½ teaspoon of crushed red pepper
5) ¼ teaspoon of salt
6) 2 (14.5 ounces) cans diced tomatoes, un-drained
7) 6 ounces whole grain farfalle pasta
8) 1 (5 ounces) white tuna solid
9) 1 Olive oil
10) 1 cup of sliced fennel

Instructions
1) Drain pasta and cook according to package instructions, avoiding salt. Return the spaghetti to the pan and cover to keep it heated. Meanwhile, drain the tuna and set aside the oil. Add additional olive oil to make 3 tbsp total if required. Set aside the flakes of tuna.
2) Heat the three tablespoons of leftover oil in a medium skillet over medium heat. Cook, stirring periodically, for 3 minutes after adding the fennel. Add the garlic, salt and simmer, crushed red pepper, constantly stirring, for approximately 1 minute, or until the garlic is golden.
3) Toss in the tomatoes. Bring to a boil, then turn off the heat. Cook, uncovered, for 5 to 6 minutes, or until the mixture thickens. Stir in the tuna and continue to cook, uncovered, for another minute or until the tuna is well heated.
4) Pour the tuna mixture over the noodles and toss to incorporate. Parsley & lemon peel should be sprinkled on top of each dish.

4.30 Chicken on a Sheet Pan with Brussels sprouts

Ready in 35 min
Servings: 4
Difficulty: Easy
Ingredients
- 1 pound of sweet potatoes, cut into 1/2-inch wedges
- ¾ teaspoon of salt
- ¾ teaspoon of ground pepper
- 4 cups quartered Brussels sprouts
- 2 tbsp of virgin olive oil
- 1 ¼ pound trimmed boneless, skinless chicken thighs
- ½ teaspoon of ground cumin
- 3 tbsp of sherry vinegar
- ½ teaspoon of dried thyme

Instructions
1) Preheat the oven to 425 ° F.
2) In a large mixing basin, toss potatoes with 1 tbsp oil and 1/4 tsp salt & pepper. On a lined baking sheet, spread evenly. 15 minutes of roasting
3) In a large mixing basin, toss Brussels sprouts with extra 1 tbsp oil and 1/4 tsp salt and pepper. On the baking sheet, mix into the sweet potatoes.
4) Season, the chicken with the other 1/4 tsp salt & pepper and cumin and thyme. Arrange the veggies on top. Roast for another 10 to 15 minutes, just until the meat is cooked through when the veggies are soft.
5) Arrange the chicken on a plate to serve. Toss the veggies with the vinegar & pour with the chicken.

4.31 Pasta e Fagioli Soup in a Slow Cooker Freezer Pack

Ready in 8 hr 15 min
Servings: 6
Difficulty: Easy
Ingredients

- 1 (15 ounces) can rinse white beans
- 4 teaspoons of dried Italian seasoning
- 4 cups of baby spinach
- 2 tbsp of extra-virgin olive oil
- ½ cup of grated Parmigiano Reggiano cheese
- 1 pound cooked of Meal-Prep Sheet-Pan Chicken
- 4 cups of cooked wheat rotini pasta
- 6 cups of sodium chicken broth
- ¼ teaspoon of salt
- 2 cups of chopped onions
- 4 tbsp of chopped freshly basil
- 1 cup of chopped celery
- 1 cup of chopped fresh carrots

Instructions

1) In a big sealable plastic bag, combine the onions, carrots, and celery. In a separate bag, combine cooled cooked chicken with cooked pasta. Refrigerate for up to five days after sealing both bags. Before starting, defrost the bags overnight in the refrigerator.

2) Fill a large slow cooker halfway with the vegetable mixture. Combine the broth, Italian seasoning, and salt in a large mixing bowl. Cook on medium for 7 1/4 hours, covered.

3) Combine the beans, spinach, and 2 tablespoons basil, when using, with the refrigerated chicken and pasta in a large mixing bowl. Cook for another 45 minutes. Into bowls, ladle the soup. Drizzle a little oil into each bowl and, if preferred, sprinkle some cheese as well as the remaining 2 tablespoons basil.

4.32 Baked Turkey Meatballs

Ready in 35 min
Servings: 3
Difficulty: Easy
Ingredients

- 1 pound of ground turkey
- 1 tbsp of chopped parsley
- ½ tbsp of chopped basil
- ½ cup of fresh Parmesan cheese
- 1 large beaten egg
- Pinch freshly grated nutmeg
- ½ cup of breadcrumbs, white/whole wheat
- 2-3 tablespoons of water or milk
- ½ tbsp of chopped oregano

Instructions

1) Preheat the oven to 350 ° F.
2) Preheat oven to 350°F. Line two baking pans with parchment paper.
3) In a large mixing bowl, crumbs, mix the turkey, cheeses, nutmeg, herbs, egg, salt & pepper, as well as the milk. Depending on how dry the bread is, you might have to vary the quantity of milk you use. The combination should be moist enough to cling together but not soggy, so it falls apart.
4) Roll pieces of the meat into 1-inch balls using only a tsp (for uniformity) or using hands, and place them on a baking sheet. You should have around 25-30 meatballs in the end.
5) Cook the meatballs for about 30 minutes, flipping once until the meat is tender through and lightly browned on both sides.

4.33 Bean Bolognese in the Crock-Pot

Ready in 4 hr
Servings: 4
Difficulty: Easy
Ingredients
- 1 chopped normal size of onion
- 2 celery chopped stalks
- 2 cloves of minced garlic
- 1 28-ounce can tomatoes
- Pasta (elective)
- 1 14-ounce can white beans
- 2 carrots chopped & peeled

Instructions

1) In a slow cooker set on low, combine all of the ingredients. Cook for 4-6 hours, or until all of the ingredients are soft. End up serving as a chunky stew (additional 12 cup water if you want a looser texture) or a sauce over cooked spaghetti.

4.34 Salmon & Cauliflower Rice Bowl for Gut Healing

Ready in 30 min
Servings: 2
Difficulty: Easy
Ingredients
- 3 tbsp olive or coconut oil
- Himalayan salt
- 1 teaspoon of sesame oil
- 1 teaspoon of curry powder
- 2 salmon fillets, sustainably sourced or organic
- ¼ cup of tamari sauce
- 1 teaspoon of Dijon mustard
- 1 teaspoon of honey
- 1 tbsp of sesame seeds
- 10 - 12 Brussels sprouts, chopped in half
- 1 bunch washed & shredded kale
- ½ head cauliflower

Instructions
1) Preheat the oven to 350 degrees Fahrenheit.
2) Spread chopped Brussels sprouts on a baking dish. Season with salt and 1 tbsp of oil. Bake for 20 minutes in the oven.
3) In the meanwhile, create the marinade by whisking together all of the ingredients in a mixing dish.
4) After 20 minutes, remove the Brussels sprouts and put the fillets in the oven pan. Return the salmon fillets to the oven for another 12 - 14 minutes, or until they are cooked to your preference.
5) Heat 1 tablespoon oil in a skillet over medium-high heat while the salmon is frying. Sauté the kale until it has reduced (2 to 3 minutes). Remove the pan from the heat and put it aside.
6) In the same pan, heat the remaining oil and add the cauliflower rice. Sauté until done, seasoning with 1 teaspoon curry powder & salt (2 to 3 minutes).
7) Take the salmon & Brussels sprouts out of the oven and divide them evenly between two dishes. Fill dishes with sautéed kale & cauliflower rice.

4.35 White Bean & Chicken Chili with Winter Vegetables

Ready in 30 min
Servings: 6
Difficulty: Easy
Ingredients
- 2 tbsp olive oil
- 1 small chopped onion
- 1 rinsed & chopped leek
- 1 seeded & diced jalapeño pepper
- 2 minced garlic cloves
- 1 tbsp of ground cumin
- Pinch of crushed red pepper flakes
- 1 large, peeled & chopped white potato
- 1 teaspoon of oregano
- 1 cup of chopped Brussels sprout

- 3 cups of chicken stock
- 1 15-ounce can small white beans
- 1 cup of milk
- 2 cups cooked, shredded chicken breast

Instructions

1) In a big saucepan, heat the olive oil over medium heat. Cook for about 5 min, till the onion & leek is translucent and tender, then mix the onion, leek, & jalapeno.
2) Add the garlic & spices to the pan and simmer for another minute, stirring constantly.
3) In a large saucepan, combine stock, white beans, the potato, Brussels sprouts and chicken. Cook, occasionally stirring, for 20 minutes, or until the potato chunks are cooked.
4) Mix in the milk & heat until it is barely warm. Serve immediately with preferred toppings.

4.36 Chicken Tenders with Harissa and Yogurt Marination

Ready in 40 min
Servings: 8
Difficulty: Easy
Ingredients
- ¼ cup of dry white wine
- 2 tbsp of Harissa paste
- 2 pounds of boneless chicken tenders
- ¼ cup of plain yogurt

Instructions

1) Combine the Harissa, yogurt, and wine in a mixing bowl. In a shallow baking dish, place the chicken tenders and cover them with the yogurt mixture. Refrigerate after wrapping with plastic wrap. Marinate for at least 2 hours and up to overnight in the refrigerator.
2) Preheat the grill for the chicken. Allow any extra marinade to drain off the chicken before removing it. Cook, the chicken for about 5 minutes on each side on a hot grill.
3) Serve with only a side salad, couscous, rice, or quinoa, or a sandwich with sliced veggies and fresh herbs.

4.37 Buffalo cauliflower baked

Ready in 35 min
Servings: 2
Difficulty: Easy
Ingredients
- 1 medium size cauliflower, cut into small pieces
- Pinch of salt & pepper
- ¼ cup of water
- ¼ cup of banana flour
- 2 tbsp of melted butter
- ½ cup of hot sauce
- For serving: ranch dressing and blue cheese

Instructions

1) Preheat oven to 425 ° F.
2) In a large mixing basin, flour mixture, water, salt, and pepper.
3) Toss the cauliflower in the flour-water mixture to coat it. Put on some kind of foil-lined baking sheet and bake for about 15 minutes, turning once.
4) In a small mixing dish, combine the butter and spicy sauce. Pour the sauce over cauliflower that has been roasted. Return the pan to the oven and bake for another 20 minutes. If preferred, serve hot with your preferred dressing on the side.

4.38 Bolognese with Polenta and Wild Mushrooms

Ready in 40 min
Servings: 4
Difficulty: Easy
Ingredients
For Polenta

- ¼ cup of Parmesan cheese
- 2 cups of yellow cornmeal
- 6 cups of vegetable stock
- 2 tbsp of unsalted butter

For Wild Mushroom Bolognese

- 6-ounces assorted wild mushrooms
- 1 teaspoon of salt
- ½ teaspoon of black pepper
- ½ cup of red wine
- 1 28-ounce can tomato
- 1 chopped fresh onion
- 2 peeled & chopped carrots
- 2 peeled & chopped celery stalks
- 2 chopped of garlic cloves
- ¼ cup of olive oil
- ½ teaspoon of dried thyme
- 1 teaspoon of dried oregano

Instructions

1) To prepare the polenta (while the Bolognese is cooking), follow these steps: Bring the water to a boil in the stock.
2) Mix in the cornmeal slowly, scraping up any clots as you need them.
3) Reduce heat to medium-low & simmer the cornmeal for 15-20 minutes or until it has thickened. It should be porridge-like inconsistency.
4) Mix in the butter & Parmesan cheese after removing the polenta from heat. Remove from the equation.
5) To create the Bolognese, onion, celery, pulse the carrots & garlic together in a food processor until finely chopped but not pureed. Remove from the equation.
6) 6. In a big saucepan, heat oil over medium heat. In the same saucepan, add the chopped veggies. Cook for about 5 minutes, or even the vegetables are soft.
7) 7. Add the mushrooms and spices to the pan. Cook for another 5 minutes, or until the mushrooms' water has drained completely.
8) 8. Add inside this red wine, grinding up any brown pieces from the bottom of the pan with a spatula.
9) 9. Bring the mixture to a boil with the tomatoes. Reduce to medium-low heat and continue to cook for another 15 minutes.
10) 10. Spoon the sauce over the polenta and serve.

4.39 Recipe for Chinese chicken salad

Ready in 25 min
Servings: 4
Difficulty: Easy
Ingredients
For Salad

- ½ cup of cilantro leaves chopped
- 2 tbsp chopped mint leaves
- ¼ cup of cooked edamame
- 4 thinly scallions sliced
- Wonton strips
- 2 cooked shredded chicken breasts (grilled)
- 1 cup of red cabbage
- 1 carrot, cut into thin pieces
- 4 cups of green cabbage

For Dressing of Salad

- 1 tbsp low-sodium soy sauce
- 1 teaspoon of sesame oil
- 2 minced garlic cloves
- ¼-inch chopped & peeled piece of ginger
- Pinch of salt
- ½ cup of vegetable oil
- ¼ cup of unseasoned rice wine vinegar
- 1 tbsp of Dijon mustard

Instructions

1) In a blender, combine all of the dressing ingredients and mix until smooth. Remove from the equation.
2) Inside a large mixing bowl, mix all of the salad ingredients. Toss the salad with the dressing. If desired, garnish with wonton strips.

4.40 Saag Paneer

Ready in 25 min
Servings: 4
Difficulty: Easy
Ingredients

- 8 ounces of paneer cheese, cut into 1/2-inch cubes
- 2 tbsp of virgin olive oil
- ¼ teaspoon of ground turmeric
- 2 cups of low-fat yogurt
- 1 finely small onion chopped
- 1 finely jalapeño pepper chopped
- 1 minced of clove garlic
- 1 tbsp of minced ginger
- 2 teaspoons of garam masala
- ¾ teaspoon of salt
- 1 teaspoon of ground cumin
- 20 ounces of chopped spinach

Instructions

1) In a medium mixing basin, mix paneer with turmeric until evenly covered in a nonstick skillet, heat 1 teaspoon oil over medium heat. Cook, tossing once until the paneer is browned on all sides, approximately 5 minutes. Place on a platter to cool.

2) In the same pan, add the rest 1 tbsp of oil. Cook, turning regularly, until golden brown, about 7 to 8 minutes, with the onion & jalapeno. (If the pan becomes dry while cooking, add 2 tbsp of water at a time.) Garlic, garam masala, ginger, & cumin are added to the pan. Cook, constantly stirring, for approximately 30 seconds, or until aromatic. Season with salt and spinach. Cook, constantly stirring, for 3 minutes, or until heated. Take the pan off the heat and add the yogurt and paneer.

4.41 Alfredo Spaghetti Squash

Ready in 35 min
Servings: 2
Difficulty: Easy
Ingredients

- 3-pound of spaghetti squash
- 1 tbsp of olive oil
- 1 cup of milk
- 2 finely garlic cloves
- 2 tbsp of brown rice flour
- 1 tbsp of yogurt
- ½ cup of Parmesan cheese
- Salt & pepper
- 1 teaspoon of dried thyme

Instructions

1) Preheat oven to 350 ° Fahrenheit.
2) Poke a few tiny holes in the squash's exterior with a knife. While roasting the squash, it will allow sufficient steam to escape, preventing it from bursting.
3) Arrange the squash on some kind of baking tray in its whole state. Bake for 45 minutes on average until the squash gets tender to the touch and the liquid has begun to drain.
4) Remove the squash from the oven and let it cool completely before slicing it lengthwise in half. Discard all of the seed as well as any fibrous parts in the center.

5) Prepare the Alfredo sauce in the meanwhile. In a saucepan over medium heat, pour in the oil.
6) Toss in the garlic and cook for about 2-3 minutes, or until fragrant.
7) Stir in the flour in the pan for about a minute to "toast" it.
8) Pour the milk into the pan, constantly whisking to incorporate the flour and scrape up any lumps.
9) Heat the milk to such a low boil, and then remove it from the heat. As it heats up, the sauce will thicken.
10) Once the sauce has reached a boil, remove it from the heat and whisk in the yogurt, Parmesan, and dried thyme. To taste, season with salt and pepper.
11) Gently "shred" the spaghetti squash halves' inside with a fork. It'll have a paste-like texture to it! The sauce should be poured over both halves.
12) Broil until the sauce is gently browned and the halves are bubbling. Remove from the oven and serve immediately.

4.42 Green Fried Rice

Ready in 20 min
Servings: 4
Difficulty: Easy
Ingredients
- 1 tbsp of olive oil
- 1 diced white onion
- ½ cup chopped broccoli
- 1 minced garlic clove
- 1 teaspoon of honey
- 2 cups of cooked brown rice
- ½ cup of frozen or fresh peas
- 1 tbsp soy sauce
- 1 diced celery stalk
- ¼ teaspoon of fresh lemon zest

Instructions
1) In an oven-safe pan, heat the olive oil over medium-high heat. Cook the vegetables, onion, and broccoli in the pan for about 2 minutes, and when the onions & celery start to soften.
2) Saute for yet another 2 minutes after adding the garlic & rice to the pan.
3) Combine the frozen peas, tamari, and honey in a mixing bowl. Cook, occasionally stirring, for a further 3-5 minutes, and when the rice is somewhat crunchy around the edges.
4) Take the pan off the heat and add the lemon zest.
5) Serve right away.

4.43 Recipe for Baked Tilapia with Pecan Rosemary Topping

Ready in 33 min
Servings: 4
Difficulty: Easy
Ingredients
- 1/3 cup of chopped pecans
- 1 egg
- 1/3 cup of whole wheat breadcrumbs
- 4 4 ounces of each tilapia fillets
- 1/2 teaspoon of coconut palm sugar
- 1 pinch of cayenne pepper
- 2 teaspoons of fresh rosemary
- 1 teaspoon of olive oil
- 1/8 teaspoon of salt

Instructions
1) Preheat the oven to 350 ° F.
2) Combine nuts, crumbs, thyme, coconut palm sugar, salt, and cayenne pepper in a small baking dish. Toss in the olive oil to cover the pecan mixture.
3) Bake for 7 to 8 minutes, or until the pecan batter is light golden brown.
4) Raise the temperature to 400 degrees Fahrenheit. Using cooking spray, coat a big glass baking dish.
5) Beat the egg white in a small bowl. Starting with one tilapia once a moment, gently cover each side of the fish with the egg yolk but then the pecan mixture.

Put the fillets inside the baking dish that has been prepared.

6) Place the leftover pecan slices on top of the tilapia fillets and press down.

7) Bake for 10 minutes, just until the tilapia is only done through. Serve the food.

4.44 Lentil Shrimp Jambalaya

Ready in 45 min
Servings: 4
Difficulty: Easy
Ingredients

- 1 cup of lentils
- 2 tbsp of butter
- 170 grams of sliced uncooked sausage
- 1 cup chopped celery, bell pepper & onion
- 3 minced garlic cloves
- 1 sliced of jalapeno
- 1 cup of tomatoes
- 1 bay leaf
- 1/2 tsp of seasoning blend Cajun creole
- 1/2 tsp of dried thyme
- 14–16 ounces peeled & deveined medium shrimp
- 1 cup of diced okra
- Sea salt & freshly black pepper
- 1 tbsp of cornstarch mixed with cold water
- Crushed red pepper flakes for gravy
- pinch of paprika

Instructions

1) First, have your lentils ready (if using uncooked lentil). To get the finest results, fully rinse the lentils beforehand. If you're using canned lentils, you may skip the cooking stage.

2) Lentils: Bring 3 cups fluid (water) to either a boil in a big saucepan. 1 1/4 cup drained and washed lentils Cover securely, lower the heat, and cook for 15-20 minutes. Drain the lentils and put them aside in a basin.

3) Heat 1 tbsp oil or butter in the same saucepan over medium to high heat. NOTE: If you're using uncooked sausage, brown it here first and then remove it. If you're using pre-cooked sausage, skip the browning and serve the shrimp and lentils with cooked sliced sausage afterward.

4) Combine the celery, onion, jalapeno, garlic and carrots/bell pepper in a large mixing bowl. To coat the pan, sauté the veggies for a few minutes on moderate to medium-high heat until the onions cook aromatic and slightly caramelized.

5) Combine the cooked lentils, smashed tomatoes, smoked paprika, Cajun spices thyme, and bay leaf in a mixing bowl. Cook until the mixture achieves a gentle simmer. Lower heat to medium-low, cover, and continue to cook for approximately 5 minutes. Simply to let the tastes mingle. Because the lentils are already cooked, you won't have to cook them for long.

6) Finally, add the shrimp and okra. Combine. Mix in a slurry of arrowroot or corn flour for a thicker jambalaya. Recombine the ingredients. Cook for 6-10 minutes on moderate, stirring either once twice or until shrimp are no longer pink. Return the saucepan to low heat and add the chicken sausage. Before serving, remove the bay leaf.

7) Toss in red pepper flakes, a pinch of sea salt, black pepper, and parsley, if preferred, and serve in bowls.

4.45 Lasagna with Tofu and Winter Squash

Ready in 50 min **Servings:** 6 **Difficulty:**Easy
Ingredients

- 2 cups of mashed winter squash like Acorn
- 1-pound of lasagna noodles
- 1 tbsp of brown sugar

- 16-ounce soft tofu
- Salt & pepper
- ½ cup of non-dairy milk like Almond or coconut
- 2 tbsp of lemon juice
- 1 tbsp of thyme leaves
- Pinch of paprika
- 4 cups of prepared Marinara sauce

Instructions

1) Preheat oven to 350°F.
2) In a large mixing bowl, combine the squash and brown sugar; put aside.
3) In a food processor, combine the tofu, lime juice, milk, thyme, & paprika and process until smooth.
4) Stir in the tofu with the squash mixture. To taste, season with salt & pepper.
5) Apply a thin layer of red sauce on the base of the 9 x 13-inch baking sheet. Add another layer of noodles on top, using about a third of the box. 1/3 of the squash & tofu filling should be on top.
6) Layer in the same sequence as before, finishing with a little quantity of the squash & tofu combination. If desired, top using bread or cracker crumbs.
7) Bake for 40 to 45 minutes, or until hot and bubbly.

4.46 Buddha Bowls with Chicken and Quinoa

Ready in 30 min
Servings: 4
Difficulty: Easy
Ingredients
Roasted Chicken Thighs
- 5 trimmed boneless, skinless chicken thighs
- ¼ teaspoon of salt
- ½ teaspoon of ground pepper

Quinoa
- 3 cups of chicken broth
- 1 cup of quinoa
- ¼ teaspoon of salt

- 1 tbsp of virgin olive oil

Italian Dressing
- 1 tbsp of sugar
- 1 tbsp of Dijon mustard
- 1 large clove of garlic
- 2 teaspoons basil, dried
- 5 tbsp water
- 2 teaspoons of oregano
- ½ teaspoon of ground pepper
- 1 ¾ cups of virgin olive oil
- ½ teaspoon of salt
- ¾ cup of vinegar

Toppings
- 1 can rinsed chickpeas
- 1 cup of sprouts
- ¼ cup of chopped nuts
- 1 sliced avocado
- 6 thinly sliced radishes

Instructions

1) To cook chicken, follow these steps: Heat the oven to 425 ° F. Place the chicken on some kind of baking pan and bake it. 1/2 teaspoon black pepper & 1/4 teaspoon salt to taste. Roast the chicken for 14 minutes, or until an immediate thermometer inserted within the thickest section registers 165 degrees F. 4 thighs, sliced.
2) Meanwhile, prepare the quinoa as follows: In a large pot, mix broth, 1 tablespoon oil, and 1/4 teaspoon salt. Bring to a boil over high heat, and then reduce to low heat. Return to low heat and stir in the quinoa. Reduce heat to low and continue to cook for 20 minutes, just until the quinoa completely absorbed all of the liquid as well as the grains have burst. Take the pan off the heat, cover it, and set it aside for 5 minutes.
3) To make the dressing, follow these steps: In a blender, combine the lemon juice, sugar, mustard, water, garlic, basil, oregano, salt and pepper. Puree until completely smooth. Slowly drizzle in the oil and purée until the mixture is creamy.

4) Assemble the bowls 3 cups quinoa, divided into 4 big shallow dishes. Sprinkle seeds over the chicken, avocado, radishes, chickpeas and sprouts. Drizzle 3/4 cup dressing on top.

4.47 Salad of Greek Kale with Quinoa and Chicken

Ready in 15 min
Servings: 2
Difficulty: Easy
Ingredients
- ¼ cup of roasted red peppers
- ¼ cup of Greek salad dressing
- 1 ounce of Crumbled cheese
- 4 cups of chopped kale
- 1 cup of shredded chicken
- 1 cup of quinoa

Instructions

1) In a large mixing bowl, combine the greens, chicken, quinoa, and roasted peppers. Toss in the dressing to coat. If preferred, top with feta cheese.

4.48 Chicken Fajita Bowls on a Sheet Pan

Ready in 40 min
Servings: 4
Difficulty: Easy
Ingredients
- 4 cups of steamed kale
- 1 can rinse no-salt-added black beans
- ¼ cup low-fat plain yogurt
- 1 tbsp of lime juice
- 2 teaspoons of water
- ½ teaspoon of smoked paprika
- ¼ teaspoon of ground pepper
- 2 tbsp of olive oil
- 1 ¼ pounds of chicken tenders
- 1 medium sliced onion
- 1 medium sliced red bell pepper
- ½ teaspoon powder of garlic
- 1 medium green bell pepper
- 2 teaspoons of chili powder
- 2 teaspoons of cumin
- ¾ teaspoon of salt

Instructions

1) Preheat the oven to 425 ° F. and place a big covered baking tray in it.
2) In a large mixing bowl, combine chili powder, cumin, a pinch of salt, garlic powder, paprika, & ground pepper. Set aside 1 teaspoon of a spice mixture in a medium bowl. In a large mixing bowl, whisk 1 tablespoon of oil into the remaining spice mixture. Toss in the chicken, onion, then red and green bell peppers.
3) Take the pan out of the oven and spray it with cooking spray. On the pan, pour the chicken combination in a uniform layer. 15 minutes of roasting.
4) In a large mixing basin, toss the kale & black beans with the remaining 1/4 teaspoon salt and 1 tbsp olive oil to coat.
5) Turn off the oven and remove the pan. Combine the chicken and veggies in a mixing bowl. Evenly distribute the greens and beans over the top. 5 to 7 minutes of roasting time till the roasted through and the veggies are soft.
6) Meanwhile, whisk together the yogurt, lemon juice, and water in the reserved spice mixture.
7) In four separate dishes, distribute the chicken & vegetable combination. Serve with a dollop of yogurt dressing on top.

Chapter 5: Snacks Recipes

5.1 Turmeric Bars

Ready in 30 min
Servings: 16 bars
Difficulty: Easy
Ingredients
For Filling

- 1/2 cup of coconut oil
- 2 teaspoon honey
- 1 1/2 teaspoon turmeric powder
- 1 teaspoon cinnamon
- 1/8 teaspoon black pepper
- 1 cup coconut butter

For Crust

- 1 cup of shredded coconut
- 1 tbsp coconut oil
- 1 teaspoon cinnamon
- 10 dates

Instructions

1) Preheat oven to 350°F and line an 8-inch four-sided baking sheet with parchment paper.
2) In a food processor, pulse the shredded coconut & dates several times until thoroughly combined. Blend in the cinnamon & coconut oil until smooth.
3) Remove the crust mixture from the bowl and place it in the pan. Press it into the pan until it's flattened evenly. Put the crust inside the refrigerator for 2-3 hours to cool.
4) Prepare the double boiler by half-filling a wide saucepot with water and bringing it

to a low boil to make the filling. To make a double boiler, lay a stainless bowl on top of the pot. Pour the coconut butter into a mixing bowl and swirl to melt it. The coconut butter should not be melted in the microwave since it will burn.

5) When the coconut butter is almost completely melted, add the coconut oil and whisk until the mixture is completely liquid.
6) Remove the pan from the heat and set it aside to rest for a few minutes.
7) Toss the filling mixture with turmeric, cinnamon, black pepper & honey.
8) Using a spoon, evenly distribute the mixture over the crust.
9) Refrigerate for 3-4 hours or overnight to harden.
10) Remove the plate from the fridge and set this on the counter for 5-10 mins after it has solidified.
11) Carefully cut into 16 squares with a sharp kitchen knife. Some could shatter, but that's ok!
12) Cinnamon should be sprinkled on top of the final bars.
13) Refrigerate & serve cold! Turmeric stains readily.

5.2 Turmeric Gummies

Ready in 4 hrs 10 min
Servings: 4
Difficulty: Easy
Ingredients

- 3 ½ cups of water
- 8 tbsp gelatin powder
- Pinch of pepper
- 1 tbsp turmeric
- 6 tbsp maple syrup

Instructions

1) Mix ground turmeric, water, & maple syrup in a big saucepan.

2) Cook for approximately 5 minutes on medium-high, often stirring to ensure that all spices are well dispersed.
3) Turn off the heat & distribute some gelatin powder over the liquid, thoroughly mixing to hydrate the gelatin.
4) Return the saucepan to heat and constantly stir with just a wooden spoon till all the gelatin has dissolved.
5) Put the liquid into a large mixing bowl and cover with plastic wrap.
6) Refrigerate the mixture for at least 4 hours or until firm.
7) When completely cooled, cut into tiny squares or any desired form and serve.

5.3 Spicy Tuna Rolls

Ready in 10 min
Servings: 6 Rolls
Difficulty: Easy
Ingredients

- 1 medium cucumber
- 1 pouch StarKist
- 1/8 teaspoon pepper
- 1/16 teaspoon cayenne
- 2 slices avocado
- 1 teaspoon hot sauce
- 1/8 teaspoon salt

Instructions

1) Finely sliced the cucumber lengthwise using a mandolin. Once the cucumber has been thinly sliced down to where the seeds emerge, turn it over and finely slice the other side. Remove the cucumber's outermost slices and any slices with seeds. With a paper towel, pat dries the leftover slices (6 total). Remove from the equation.
2) Combine tuna, spicy sauce, salt, pepper, & cayenne in a small mixing bowl. Mix until all of the ingredients are well combined.

3) Spoon tuna mixture over cucumber slices one at a time, leaving one inch per side. Place one slice of avocado over the tuna, then wrap the cucumber up gently, closing the end with two toothpicks.

5.4 Mixed Nuts with Ginger Spice

Ready in 45 min
Servings: 8
Difficulty: Easy
Ingredients

- 2 egg whites
- 1 teaspoon ginger
- 1/2 teaspoon fine sea salt
- 2 cups mixed nuts, cashew, raw almonds, goji berries, pumpkin seeds, etc.
- 1/2 teaspoon cinnamon
- Coconut oil spray
- Parchment paper

Instructions

1) Preheat the oven to 250 degrees Fahrenheit.
2) Whisk the egg whites until they are foamy. Grate the ginger, season with fine sea salt, and sprinkle with Vietnamese cinnamon. Whip the ingredients until it is well mixed.
3) Toss in your favorite raw mixed nuts into the egg white combination. Toss to coat.
4) Lightly mist the parchment paper using coconut oil spray. On the baking sheet, equally, distribute the nuts. Bake at 250 degrees Fahrenheit for 40 minutes, or until fragrant, rotating the baking sheet pan halfway through.
5) Break the combined nuts into pieces after they have cooled and stiffened. Keep the container sealed. Keep them in the fridge if the temperature is high.

5.5 Spicy Kale Chips

Ready in 26 min
Servings: 4
Difficulty: Easy
Ingredients

- 1 cluster of curly kale
- spray oil
- 1/8 teaspoon garlic powder
- 1/4 teaspoon sea salt
- 1/4 teaspoon of cayenne pepper
- 1/8 teaspoon black pepper

Instructions

1) Preheat oven to 300 ° F.
2) Thoroughly rinse your kale. Air dry, blow dry inside a salad spinner, and pat dry with paper towels are all options.
3) Cut kale leaves from their stems/ribs into potato chip-sized pieces.
4) Arrange on a wire cooling rack, spaced apart, on top of a foil-lined cookie sheet.
5) If you're cooking a lot of kale, divide it into two sheets or batches, so it cooks evenly.
6) Delicately spritz with such a simple cooking spray or lightly massage a little amount of oil into kale leaves with your fingertips. To make crispy kale chips, gently cover the leaves in oil without putting too much moisture on them. In addition, its wire baking rack guarantees that the crisp factor is maximized.
7) Pinch of salt, garlic powder, & cayenne pepper. They'll be spicier if you add extra cayenne pepper. Do you want them to be mild? Instead of cayenne pepper, use sweet paprika!
8) Bake for 18-20 minutes on the middle rack or until the edges are crisp.

5.6 Ginger Date Bars

Ready in 20 min **Servings:** 8 Bars
Difficulty: Easy
Ingredients

- ¼ cup of almond milk
- 1 teaspoon of ground ginger
- 1 ½ cup almonds
- ¾ cup of dates

Instructions

1) Preheat oven to 350 ° degrees Fahrenheit.
2) To produce the almond flour, pulse the almonds for about 1-2 minutes in a high-powered blender until fine and powdery. If you stir the almonds too much, they'll start to leak their oils, ending in nut butter. Remove from the equation.
3) To prepare the date paste, combine the dates and almond milk in the same blender and puree for around 3-5 minutes, or till you have a puree.
4) Blend the date mixture for 2-3 minutes with the almond flour & powdered ginger.
5) Pour the sauce into an oven-safe baking dish & bake for 20 minutes.
6) Allow it cool before slicing into eight bars of similar size.

5.7 Orange Juice with Vanilla and Turmeric

Ready in 5 min
Servings: 2
Difficulty: Easy
Ingredients

- 3 peeled oranges
- Pinch of pepper
- 1 t vanilla extract
- 1 cup of almond milk
- ½ teaspoon of cinnamon
- ¼ tbsp turmeric

Instructions

1) In a blender, combine all of the ingredients.
2) Puree until smooth, and then strain into a glass to serve.

5.8 Gelatin Gummies with Hibiscus and Ginger

Ready in 12 min
Servings: 28 Gummies
Difficulty: Easy

Ingredients

- 1 cup of water
- 1 teaspoon ginger juice
- 2 tbsp gelatin powder
- 3 tbsp hibiscus flowers cut
- 1½ tbsp honey

Instructions

1) In a small saucepan, bring water to a boil.
2) Turn off the heat and stir in the hibiscus blossoms.
3) Cover and set aside for 5 minutes to infuse.
4) Using a tiny sieve, drain the flowers.
5) Restore the liquid to a saucepan, add the honey and ginger, and whisk to combine.
6) Scatter the gelatin over the surface of the liquid and wait for it to soften & dissolve. After several minutes, whisk to ensure that gelatin is completely dissolved and there are no clumps.
7) Pour into the silicone mold right away (or a rectangular baking dish creased with parchment paper).
8) Allow cooling before placing in the refrigerator for at least two h.
9) To remove your gummies from the mold, just press down on the bottom of the mold with your fingertips.
10) Welcome to the table.

5.9 Baked Turmeric Veggie Nuggets

Ready in 35 min
Servings: 24 Nuggets
Difficulty: Easy

Ingredients

- 1 cup of chopped carrots
- 1 tbsp garlic
- 2 cups of cauliflower florets
- 2 cups of broccoli florets
- 1/2 teaspoon ground turmeric
- 1/2 cup of almond meal
- 1 pasture-raised egg
- 1/4 teaspoon sea salt
- 1/4 tbsp black pepper

Instructions

1) Preheat oven to 400 degrees Fahrenheit and line a pan with parchment paper.
2) In a food processor, mix the carrots, garlic, cauliflower, turmeric, sea salt, broccoli, and black pepper. Pulse until the mixture is fine.
3) Pulse in the almond meal & egg until barely combined.
4) Pour into a mixing basin. Scoop out a spoonful of the ingredients and shape them into round discs with your palms. Place on a baking sheet that has been lined with parchment paper.
5) Cook for 25 minutes, rotating halfway through. For dipping, serve additional Paleo ranch sauce.

5.10 Slaw with Pineapple & Ginger Cream

Ready in 40 min **Servings:** 12 +**Difficulty:** Easy
Ingredients
Pineapple Slaw

- 1/2 slice of red cabbage
- 2 red peppers
- 3 cups pineapple chunks
- 1 cup chopped cilantro
- 1/2 head green cabbage

Creamy Ginger Sauce

- 1 cup of soaked cashews
- 1/2 teaspoon of red pepper flakes
- salt and pepper
- 1/2 cup of water
- 2 teaspoon lime juice
- 2 inches ginger

Instructions

1) Put cashews in a mixing bowl. Fill the container halfway with water. Allow for at least 30 minutes of soak time, preferably up overnight.
2) Begin preparing the sauce. The cashews should be drained and rinsed. In a high-powered blender or food processor, combine the soaked cashews and the additional sauce ingredients.
3) In a large mixing bowl, combine the red peppers, cabbage, & pineapple. Mix in the sauce well. Stir in the cilantro until it is well incorporated.
4) Have fun.

5.11 Muffins with Turmeric & Coconut Flour

Ready in 30 min **Servings:** 8 Muffins
Difficulty: Easy

Ingredients

- 1 teaspoon of vanilla extract
- 2 tbsp of coconut flour
- ½ teaspoon of baking soda
- 2 teaspoon of turmeric
- 6 eggs
- ½ cup of coconut milk
- ⅓ cup of maple syrup
- ½ teaspoon of ginger powder
- salt and pepper

Instructions

1) Preheat oven to 350 degrees Fahrenheit. Make 8 muffin liners in a muffin tray.
2) Combine eggs, maple syrup, milk & vanilla extract in a large mixing basin. Blend until everything is fully blended and the eggs start to bubble.
3) Sift up coconut flour, turmeric, ginger powder, baking soda, pepper, & salt in a small basin.
4) Gradually whisk in the dry ingredients till the mixture is smooth and thick.
5) Divide the batter equally among the muffin cups in the prepared muffin tray.
6) Cook for 25 minutes, or until the edges are gently browned.
7) Remove the muffins out from the oven and cool on a wire rack.

5.12 No-Bake Golden Turmeric Energy Bites

Ready in 5 hrs 20 min
Servings: 18 Bites
Difficulty: Easy
Ingredients

- 1 cup almond
- ½ teaspoon maple syrup
- 2 teaspoon turmeric
- 3/4 coconut flakes
- 4-6 tbsp plant-based protein powder
- 1 teaspoon coconut oil

Instructions

1) Blend nut butter, 12 coconut oil, maple syrup, almond butter, coconut flakes, protein powder, and turmeric in a blender.
2) In a high-powered blender, combine all of the ingredients until they're uniformly dispersed.
3) Allow 30-60 minutes for the dough to solidify in the refrigerator.
4) Take the dough out of the fridge and shape it into 12-inch diameter bite-sized balls.
5) Place the balls on a parchment-lined dish and chill for 3-4 hours.
6) Take it out of the fridge. Toss the ball in the remaining crushed coconut on a dish. Enjoy.

5.13 Coconut Oil with Turmeric Ginger Smoothie

Ready in 5 min
Servings: 1
Difficulty: Easy
Ingredients

- 1 teaspoon of turmeric
- 1 teaspoon of chia seeds
- 1 cup ice
- 1 tbsp of coconut oil
- 2 tbsp pure
- 1½ cups of coconut milk
- 1 teaspoon of ginger

Instructions

1) In a blender, combine the ice, turmeric, coconut oil, coconut milk, honey, and ginger. Blend on high until the mixture is smooth and frosty.
2) Dilute into a glass & add chia seeds to taste. Allow a few minutes for the chia seeds to grow before drinking.

5.14 Banana Ginger Coconut Flour Bars

Ready in 10 min
Servings: 1
Difficulty: Easy
Ingredients

- ⅓ cup of raw honey
- 6 eggs
- 1½ tbsp of ginger
- 2 tbsp of cinnamon
- 3 small of bananas
- 1 cup of coconut flour
- ⅓ cup of coconut oil
- 1 teaspoon of ground cardamom
- 1 teaspoon of baking soda
- 2 teaspoon of apple vinegar

Instructions

1) Preheat oven to 350 ° degrees Fahrenheit. Grease or line a 9x9 glass baking sheet with parchment paper.
2) 2. In a food processor, add all ingredients and process until smooth. Combine the baking soda and vinegar in a blender until smooth, then drop into the prepared dish.
3) 3. Bake for 30-40 minutes, or until a toothpick inserted in the center comes out clean.

5.15 Kombucha Gummies for Gut Healing

Ready in 3 hrs 25 min
Servings: 25 Gummies
Difficulty: Easy
Ingredients

- 1 teaspoon grated ginger
- 6 tbsp honey
- 1/3 cup of gelatin powder
- 1 ½ cups kombucha
- 1/2 cup of grapefruit juice
- 1 tbsp grapefruit zest

Instructions

1) Use plastic wrap to line the bottom of just a 9x9-inch glass pan.
2) Bring a medium saucepan of water to a boil with the grated ginger. Allow for a five-minute boil to destroy the protease enzymes in the ginger. Drain the water and put it aside.
3) Mix the kombucha, zest, grapefruit juice, & honey in a large pot and stir thoroughly. Spread the gelatin powder on top and set aside for a few minutes to hydrate.
4) Reduce the heat to medium-low & slowly simmer the mixture until the gelatin powder melts. Mix until the entire gelatin has dissolved.
5) In a blender, pulse the gelatin mixture as well as the boiling grated ginger for 20 seconds.
6) Chill the mixture for at least 3 hours until it's solid in the prepared glass pan. After that, cut the cake into little pieces and serve!

5.16 Spicy Nuts

Ready in 20 min
Servings: 6 Snacks
Difficulty: Easy
Ingredients
- 1 cup almonds
- 1.5 teaspoon chili powder
- 1/2 teaspoon garlic powder
- 1 cup of pecans
- 1 cup of cashews
- 1/2 teaspoon cumin
- 1/4 teaspoon cayenne pepper
- 1 tbsp olive oil
- 1/2 teaspoon black pepper
- 1/2 teaspoon sea salt

Instructions

1) Preheat the oven to 350°F and prepare a baking sheet with parchment paper. On the baking pan, arrange the nuts in a single layer. Preheat oven to 350°F and roast for 15 min, flipping halfway.
2) In a small bowl, combine chili powder, cumin, black pepper, salt, and cayenne pepper while the nuts are roasting.
3) Remove the nuts from the oven and set them aside to cool. With a mixing dish, coat the nuts with olive oil and in the spice mixture.
4) Keep at room temperature in an airtight container.

5.17 Gummies with Apple Cider Vinegar

Ready in 1 hr 10 min
Servings: 24
Difficulty: Easy
Ingredients
- 1 ½ cup apple juice
- ½ cup of apple cider vinegar
- ½ cup of water
- 5 tbsp gelatin powder

Instructions

1) In a large saucepan over low heat, mix the apple cider vinegar, apple juice, and water and whisk thoroughly. Mix in the gelatin powder with the liquid and set aside for two minutes.
2) Reduce the heat to low and constantly whisk for five minutes until the gelatin gets completely dissolved.
3) Fill ice cube trays halfway with gelatin mixture and place in the fridge 1 hr earlier serving.

5.18 Protein Bars with Cacao Coffee

Ready in 10 min
Servings: 12
Difficulty: Easy
Ingredients
- 2 cups nut 1 cup egg white protein powder
- 1/4 cup cacao powder

- 1/4 cup cacao nibs
- 3 tbsp instant coffee
- 18 large Medjool dates
- 3–5 tbsp water

Instructions

1) Preheat oven to 350°F. Line an 8-inch square baking sheet with just a square silicone baking pan; put aside.

2) Mix egg white protein, nuts, cacao powder, and coffee powder in a food processor bowl until nuts are broken down into tiny bits. It's important not to over-process the nuts since they'll try to set down in the following stage.

3) Add the pitted dates and blend until smooth–the mixture may seem dry at this point. 1 tsp of water at a time, with the engine running, until the mixture is thick and all comes together. You would need less or more water depending on whether your dates are juicy or dry. I used a total of 6 tablespoons.

4) Remove S-blade and whisk in cacao nibs if using after the mixture has come together, which is sticky.

5) Pour the mixture into an 8-inch square pan that has been lined with parchment paper. Push evenly into the pan with somewhat damp palms. To get it extra flat, I use his adorable tiny pastry roller.

6) Chill for 1 hour or freeze for 30 min before chopping into bars in the pan.

5.19 Recipe for Lemon-Blueberry Bread

Ready in 1 hr 5 min **Servings:** 16
Difficulty: Easy
Ingredients
- 1 cup Knudsen Sour Cream
- 1/2 cup of oil

- 1 teaspoon lemon zest
- 1/2 teaspoon vanilla
- 1 cup blueberries
- 1-1/2 cups plus 1 tbsp flour
- 2 teaspoon baking powder
- 1/2 teaspoon salt
- 3 eggs
- 1 cup of sugar

Instructions
1) Preheat the oven to 350 degrees Fahrenheit.

2) In a large mixing basin, mix baking soda, 1-1/2 cups flour, and salt. Whisk together the sour cream, oil, sugar, lemon zest, eggs, and vanilla extract until well combined. Pour to flour mixture and whisk until just combined.

3) Toss the blueberries with the remaining flour and gently fold them into the batter. Fill an oiled & greased 9x5-inch loaf pan halfway with batter.

4) 1 hour to 1 hour 5 minutes in the oven, or until a toothpick inserted in the middle comes out clean. Allow 10 minutes for cooling. Then, remove the bread from the pan and place it on a wire rack to cool it entirely.

5.20 Shortbread Cookies with Lavender

Ready in 40 min **Servings:** 4-8
Difficulty: Easy
Ingredients
- 1/2 cup ghee
- 1/4 cup coconut oil
- 1/4 cup of maple syrup
- 1/4 teaspoon sea salt
- 1 teaspoon lemon zest
- 1/4 cup honey
- 1 cup of cassava flour
- 1/4 cup of nut flour
- 1/2 cup of arrowroot flour
- 1/4 cup of coconut flour
- 1 teaspoon dried lavender food grade

Instructions

1) In a large mixing bowl, combine the dry ingredients. Cream together ghee, maple syrup, coconut oil, & honey in a separate bowl. Combine the wet and dry ingredients in a mixing bowl. Mix until everything is properly combined.

2) Roll dough into a 2-inch-diameter log & freeze for 15-30 min, or until solid. A baking sheet should be greased.

3) Heat the oven to 325 ° F. Slice the cookies 1/4-inch thick & space them approximately an inch apart on the prepared baking sheet.

4) Bake or until the sides are browning and the bottoms of the cookies are crisp and golden.

5.21 Energy Balls

Ready in 15 min **Servings:** 23 Balls
Difficulty: Easy
Ingredients
- 1/4 cup of sunflower seeds
- 2 tbsp chia seeds
- 2 tbsp ground flaxseeds
- 3/4 cup Medjool dates
- 3/4 cup of almonds
- 3/4 cup chopped dried fruit
- 1/2 teaspoon vanilla extract
- 1/4 teaspoon cinnamon

Instructions

1) Set aside a sheet pan lined with parchment paper.

2) Mix the pitted dates & almonds in the food processor. Pulse until the mixture resembles coarse crumbs.

3) Combine the remaining ingredients in a food processor and mix until smooth. The paste should be thick and readily stick together when two fingers are pressed together. Adding 1 tbsp of freshwater if the batter seems dry.

4) A spoonful of the ingredients should be rolled into a 1-inch ball. Rep till all the mixture is already rolled out on the prepared sheet pan.

5) Refrigerate the balls for approximately an hour until once they are firm. Refrigerate in an airtight container. This recipe makes 20-23 balls.

5.22 Peanut Butter Chocolate Chex Bars

Ready in 45 min **Servings:** 32
Difficulty: Easy
Ingredients
- 1 cup of corn syrup
- 6 cups of Honey Nut cereal
- 1 bag of milky chocolate chips
- 2 tbsp butter
- 1 cup of sugar
- 1 1/4 cups of butter peanut
- 1/4 teaspoon of salt

Instructions

1) Coat a 13x9-inch baking pan using cooking spray.

2) Microwave corn syrup & sugar, uncovered, on High 2 min 30 seconds, mixing every 30 seconds, until the liquid just starts to boil in a large microwaveable basin.

3) Mix in 1 cup of peanut butter as well as the salt until well combined.

4) Toss in the grains until it is uniformly covered. Make sure the surface is even by pressing the mixture firmly into the pan.

5) Heat chocolate chips, leftover 1/4 cup peanut butter, and butter uncovered in a medium microwaveable dish for 1 minute on high; stir until smooth. Distribute across the bars.

6) Refrigerate for at least 30 minutes or until the chocolate has hardened. Cut 8 lines by 4 rows for the bars.

5.23 Salad with Asparagus and Artichokes

Ready in 20 min
Servings: 4
Difficulty: Easy
Ingredients
- 2 tbsp Dr. Sears' Zone Virgin Olive Oil
- 1 teaspoon of Garlic powder
- 1-pint of cherry tomatoes
- 1 can Artichoke hearts canned in water
- 3 slices of red onion
- 3 tbsp of lemon juice
- 1 1/4 pounds of asparagus
- Salt and pepper

Instructions

1) Soak the onions in lime juice in a large mixing dish. Remove from the equation.
2) Preheat the microwave to 400 degrees Fahrenheit.
3) Cut off the rough ends of the asparagus bottoms (approximately 1/2 to 1 inch). Season the asparagus stalks with salt and olive oil frying spray.
4) Place on a foil-lined baking dish in a single layer and roast for 8-10 minutes, or until lightly browned & fork tender.

5) Take the asparagus out of the oven and chop it into little pieces.
6) Combine the asparagus, the other ingredients, including the onions including lemon juice, in a mixing dish. To blend, stir everything together.
7) Serve at room temperature or cooled.

5.24 Yogurt with Almonds and Blueberries

Ready in 5 min
Servings: 1
Difficulty: Easy

Ingredients
- 2 teaspoon Slivered almonds
- 1/4 cup 0 Greek yogurt
- 1/3 cup of Blueberries

Instructions

1) Mix all materials in a bowl & enjoy.

5.25 Cottage Cheese with Applesauce

Ready in 5 min
Servings: 1
Difficulty: Easy
Ingredients
- Cinnamon and ginger
- 2 teaspoon Almonds
- 1/4 cup Applesauce
- 1/4 cup cottage cheese

Instructions
1) Combine applesauce as well as cottage cheese in a mixing bowl.
2) Cinnamon and ginger should be sprinkled on top.
3) Serve with sliced almonds on top.

5.26 Sauce for Barbecue

Ready in 45 min
Servings: 4
Difficulty: Easy
Ingredients
- 1 teaspoon of Worcestershire sauce
- 3/4 cup of Chicken stock
- 3 tbsp of cider vinegar
- 1 cup of tomato puree
- 1/3 cup of applesauce
- 1 tbsp of liquid smoke
- 4 teaspoon of garlic
- 1/4 teaspoon of chili powder
- 4 teaspoon of cornstarch

Instructions
1) To make the sauce, combine all of the components in a small pot. (Before adding cornstarch to the pot, mix it with some cold water to dissolve it.)
2) Warm sauce to a low simmer, stirring regularly with either a whisk until everything thickens.
3) Transfer the sauce to a container, set aside to cool, and the fridge.

5.27 Freezer Pops of Berries

Ready in 5 min/Overnight
Servings: 6
Difficulty: Easy

Ingredients
- 1 cup of Strawberries
- 3 cups of yogurt
- 1 1/2 tbsp of almonds

Instructions
1) In a food processor, combine the strawberries and almonds until they are very minute bits.
2) Pulse some few times to incorporate the yogurt.
3) Divide the yogurt mixture evenly into 6 tiny paper cups.

4) In the center of the yogurt, place a Popsicle stick.
5) Place in the freezer for at least one night.
6) Remove the paper cup before eating.

5.28 Berry good snack

Ready in 5 min
Servings: 1
Difficulty: Easy
Ingredients
- 1 teaspoon of Walnuts
- Stevia for taste
- 5 Blueberries
- 1 teaspoon of Vanilla
- 5 Strawberries
- 1/4 cup of ricotta cheese
- 1 teaspoon of lemon juice

Instructions
1) Set aside strawberries that have been cleaned and hulled.
2) Ricotta, lemon juice, vanilla, crumbled walnuts, and stevia are combined in a mixing bowl.
3) Top each strawberry with a spoonful of the ricotta mixture.
4) Sprinkle each strawberry with just blueberry and put them in a dish on their sides to form a star, with the blueberry in the center and strawberries on the edges.

5.29 Salad with Blackberries and Shrimp

Ready in 10 min
Servings: 1
Difficulty: Easy
Ingredients
- 2 drops of Agave Nectar
- 1/2 cup of Baby Spinach
- 1/2 teaspoon of Dr. Sears' Virgin Olive Oil
- 2 teaspoon of Lemon Juice
- 1/2 cup of chopped Yellow Bell Pepper

- Salt and Pepper
- 1/2 cup of Blackberries
- 2 chopped medium Shrimp

Instructions
1) To prepare the dressing, mix olive oil, lemon juice, and agave nectar using a fork.
2) Transfer the spinach & bell peppers to a salad dish and toss with the dressing.
3) Serve with blackberries & shrimp on the side.

5.30 Breakfast with Blueberries and Yogurt

Ready in 5 min
Servings: 1
Difficulty: Easy
Ingredients
- 1 cup of Strawberries
- 1 cup of yogurt
- 2 tbsp of Walnuts
- 3/4 cup of Blueberries

Instructions
1) Stir fruits & nuts into the yogurt.

5.31 Brussels Sprouts in a Garlic-Black Bean Sauce

Ready in 15 min
Servings: 3
Difficulty: Easy
Ingredients
- 2 1/2 cups of Brussels sprouts
- black pepper
- 1 1/2 teaspoon of Dr. Sears' Zone Extra Virgin Olive Oil
- 1/2 teaspoon of red pepper flakes
- 1 1/2 tbsp of Black bean garlic sauce

Instructions
1) The Brussels sprouts should be quartered lengthwise.

2) In a large pan, heat the oil and chili flakes over medium-high heat.
3) Cook the Brussels sprouts in the pan for approximately 3-5 minutes or until they start to color a little. They may absorb all of the oil. If this is the case, add a spoonful of water or broth.
4) Stir throughout black bean garlic sauce until all of the Brussels sprouts are thoroughly covered.
5) Add a dash of black pepper to taste. Cook for a further 30 seconds.
6) Remove from the heat and serve right away.

5.32 Strawberries and Cacao Greek Yogurt

Ready in 5 min
Servings: 1
Difficulty: Easy
Ingredients
- 1/4 cup of Greek yogurt
- 2 teaspoon of Almonds
- 1 1/2 tbsp of Cacao Powder
- 1/4 cup of Strawberries

Instructions
1) In a mixing bowl, combine the Greek yogurt and cacao powder.
2) Blend in the strawberries & almonds gently.

5.33 Dirty Rice in Cajun Style

Ready in 20 min
Servings: 4
Difficulty: Easy
Ingredients
- 2 teaspoon of Dr. Sears' Zone Virgin Olive Oil
- 1 cup of green bell pepper
- 1 cup of red bell pepper
- 3 cups of Cauliflower
- 1 teaspoon of fresh thyme
- 1 Bay leaf

- Salt and pepper
- 4 cloves of Garlic
- 1 cup of white onion
- 2 chopped celery stalks
- 3 tbsp of unsalted vegetable stock
- 1/2 teaspoon of Chili powder
- 1/2 teaspoon of Cumin

Instructions

1) In a large skillet, heat the olive oil on medium heat.
2) Sauté the garlic, onion, celery, & peppers until they are tender.
3) Add the rice cauliflower, thyme, bay leaf, chili, salt, pepper, and cumin, and stir to combine.
4) To combine the flavors, add a tiny quantity of stock (1 tbsp at a time).

5.34 Dressing with Carrots and Ginger

Ready in 10 min
Servings: 8 tbsp of servings
Difficulty: Easy
Ingredients

- 3 tbsp of soy sauce low sodium
- 2 tbsp of Ginger root
- 1 tbsp of Sesame oil
- 2 Carrots
- 1/4 cup of vinegar
- 2 teaspoon of Virgin Olive Oil
- 1/4 cup of Water
- 1 tbsp of Tahini
- For taste Stevia

Instructions

1) In a blender, puree everything except the carrots.
2) Add the carrots just a few pieces to the blender while it's running and mix till smooth before pouring more.
3) If the dressing is too thick, add 2 teaspoons of water at a time until you get the appropriate consistency.

5.35 Popcorn made with cauliflower

Ready in 35 min
Servings: 1
Difficulty: Easy
Ingredients

- 2 teaspoon of Olive oil
- 4 cups of cauliflower
- Salt for taste

Instructions

1) Cut into buds after removing the core.
2) Toss to coat with olive oil.
3) Season to taste with a good quantity of salt.
4) Roast at 450°F for 25-30 minutes.
5) Drizzle with virgin olive oil before serving.

5.36 Cauliflower-Mash

Ready in 15 min
Servings: 2
Difficulty: Easy
Ingredients

- 1 16-oz of bag cauliflower
- 1 teaspoon of Dr. Sears' Zone Virgin Olive Oil
- Salt and Pepper
- 2 tbsp of chicken stock
- 3 1/2 tbsp of Greek yogurt

Instructions

1) Microwave the cauliflower in the stock for 10 - 15 minutes, or until it's cooked but still crisp, not mushy.
2) In a blender, stick blender, or food processor, purée all of the ingredients, except the olive oil, until they have the texture of mashed potatoes.
3) Pour with the olive oil before serving.

5.37 Hummus with celery

Ready in 5 min
Servings: 1
Difficulty: Easy
Ingredients
- 2 tbsp of Hummus spread
- 6 stalks Celery
- 3 tbsp of Salsa
- 1 oz of chicken breast cooked

Instructions
1) Fill the celery stalks' wells with hummus and chicken bits.
2) Cut chicken into hummus, then use the celery as a spoon if you wish.

5.38 Chard Salad with Parmesan

Ready in 20 min
Servings: 4
Difficulty: Easy
Ingredients
- 3 tbsp of Lemon Juice
- 1 1/2 tbsp of Virgin Olive Oil
- 1/2 cup of Parmesan (grated)
- Pepper
- 2 tbsp of Water
- 2 teaspoons of Lemon Zest
- 1/4 teaspoon of salt
- 1/2 teaspoon of Garlic Powder

Instructions
1) Remove the stems from the chard and coarsely chop them, leaving the leaves alone.
2) In a small bowl, mix the lemon zest, water, lemon juice, 1/4 teaspoon salt, and garlic powder to form a dressing. Whisk in the olive oil slowly. Remove from the equation.
3) Toss the chard stems & leaves firmly with the Parmesan & roughly 2/3 of the lime dressing in a large mixing basin; serve the remainder on the side.
4) Season with black pepper to taste.

5.39 Plum & Cheese Snack

Ready in 25 min
Servings: 4
Difficulty: Easy
Ingredients
- 1 Low-fat of cheese stick
- 1 Plum

Instructions
1) Mix these two ingredients.

5.40 Lemon Zucchini with Cheesy Sauce

Ready in 20 min
Servings: 4
Difficulty: Easy

Ingredients
- 2 teaspoons of dried oregano
- 3 lbs. of Zucchini
- 1/2 teaspoon of Lemon zest
- 1/2 teaspoon of pepper flakes red
- Cooking spray, olive oil
- 2 teaspoons of Virgin Olive Oil
- 1/4 teaspoon of Cayenne pepper
- 2 oz Fat-free creamy cheese
- 2 tbsp of vegetable stock
- Salt and pepper

Instructions

1) Cooking oil should be sprayed onto a pan. In a large pan, heat the olive oil over high heat and add the zucchini, lemon zest, & red pepper flakes.
2) Cook for another 2 minutes, adding more stock if necessary.
3) Continue cooking until zucchini is soft, approximately 5 minutes, after adding salt, black pepper, & cayenne pepper.
4) Add cheese into zucchini combination and simmer for 1 minute, or until cream cheese starts to melt.
5) Remove the pan from the heat and add the oregano.

5.41 Fruit & Cottage Cheese

Ready in 5 min
Servings: 1
Difficulty: Easy
Ingredients
- 1/3 cup of Mandarin oranges
- 1 1/2 teaspoon of Slivered almonds
- 1/4 cup of cheese Low-fat cottage

Instructions

1) Mix the mandarin orange sections in a bowl with the low-fat cottage cheese.
2) Top with slivered or sliced almonds.

5.42 Chicken Gravy with a Country Flair

Ready in 25 min
Servings: 3 Cups
Difficulty: Easy
Ingredients
- 2 1/2 cups of chicken stock
- 1/2 teaspoon of Garlic
- 1/2 teaspoon of Celery salt
- 2 1/2 cups of Onions
- 6 teaspoons of Cornstarch
- 1 tbsp of White wine
- 1 teaspoon of Parsley flakes
- 1 teaspoon salt and pepper for taste

Instructions

1) Mix all of the ingredients.

5.43 Yogurt with cucumber and cashews

Ready in 5 min
Servings: 1
Difficulty: Easy
Ingredients
- 1 cup of Cucumber
- 1/4 cup of Greek yogurt
- 2 teaspoons of Cashews
- 2 teaspoon of squeezed lemon juice
- 1 teaspoon of chopped fresh dill

Instructions

1) Cucumbers should be sliced.
2) Combine yogurt, cashews, lemon juice, and dill in a mixing bowl.

5.44 Cucumber Cups

Ready in 10 min
Servings: 3
Difficulty: Easy
Ingredients
- 1 cucumber
- 1/4 cup of sour cream
- 1 tbsp of Horseradish mustard
- 1 sprig fresh dill
- 1/3 cup of Hummus
- 6 halved of Cherry tomatoes

Instructions

1) Split the cucumber into 12 pieces using a knife.
2) Cut the cherry tomatoes in half.
3) Scoop out the interior meat, being cautious not to go all the way to the bottom with your scoop.
4) Drain the pieces on paper towels or cotton towels.
5) In the meanwhile, mix the mustard & sour cream until smooth and put aside.
6) 1 teaspoon of hummus in each cup, followed by the sour cream mix.
7) Serve with a dill sprig as a garnish.

5.45 Hummus-Dipped Devilled Eggs

Ready in 15 min
Servings: 1
Difficulty: Easy
Ingredients

- 2 Egg
- 4 tbsp of Hummus
- Paprika to taste

Instructions

1) Slice the eggs in half, discard yolks, and fill each egg white half with one-fourth of the hummus.
2) Top with paprika to taste.

5.46 Dill Sauce

Ready in 15 min
Servings: 1
Difficulty: Easy
Ingredients

- 3/4 teaspoon of Virgin Olive Oil
- 1 teaspoon of Garlic
- 1 teaspoon dill
- 1/3 cup of Greek yogurt
- 2 teaspoons of dry white wine
- Salt and pepper
- 1 1/2 teaspoon of Cornstarch

Instructions

1) Combine yogurt, white wine, garlic, olive oil, & dill in a small saucepan. Reduce the heat to a low setting. Boiling is not recommended.
2) Combine the cornstarch and a little water to make a slur (thin paste).
3) Frequently whisk the cornstarch mix into the yogurt. Return to very low heat after bringing to a simmer (when the sauces will thicken). Boiling is not recommended.
4)

5.47 Easy Creamy Spinach Dip

Ready in 25 min
Servings: 5
Difficulty: Easy
Ingredients

- 1 tbsp Shallot
- 1/2 cup of cottage cheese
- 1/4 cup of Greek yogurt
- 1 tbsp of lemon juice
- 1 (5 oz) can Water chestnuts
- 1/3 cup of cream
- 1/2 teaspoon of salt
- Black pepper - to taste
- Zone-favorable vegetables for dipping
- 8 oz Baby spinach
- 2 tbsp fresh chives

Instructions

1) In a food processor, roughly chop the shallot and water chestnuts.
2) Pulse together the cream cheese, yogurt, lemon juice, cottage cheese, salt, and pepper until well blended.
3) Pulse in the spinach & chives until well combined.
4) Cut up some Zone-friendly vegetables, and you're good to go.

5.48 Eggplant Caviar

Ready in 30 min
Servings: 4
Difficulty: Easy
Ingredients

- 2 1/2 lbs. Eggplants (same size)
- 1/2 cup of Scallions
- 1 tbsp of lemon juice
- 1/2 teaspoon of dried basil leaves
- 2 cloves of Garlic
- 2 tbsp of vegetable stock
- Black pepper
- 2 1/2 teaspoon of Virgin Olive Oil

Instructions

1) Preheat the oven to 400 degrees Fahrenheit (or grill).
2) Cut the eggplants in half lengthwise and set them cut-side down on a baking pan. Preheat oven to 350°F and bake for 20 minutes, or until fork-tender.
3) In a blender or food processor, purée the pulp from the skin.
4) Blend in the other ingredients, except the olive oil, until smooth.
5) Add the olive oil and mix well.
6) Chill for 1 hour or serve at room temperature.

My Recipes And Notes

Mo	Tu	We	Th	Fr	Sa	Su

Recipe Name _____

Preparation Time: Serving: Difficulty Level:

Ingredients

....
....
....
....
....
....

Steps for preparation

_____
_____
_____
_____
_____
_____
_____
_____

Recipe Name _____

Preparation Time: Serving: Difficulty Level:

Ingredients

....
....
....
....
....
....

Steps for preparation

_____
_____
_____
_____
_____
_____
_____
_____

Recipe Name _____

Preparation Time: Serving: Difficulty Level:

Ingredients

....
....
....
....
....
....

Steps for preparation

_____
_____
_____
_____
_____
_____
_____
_____

Recipe Name _____

Preparation Time: Serving: Difficulty Level:

Ingredients

....
....
....
....
....
....

Steps for preparation

_____
_____
_____
_____
_____
_____
_____
_____

Recipe Name _____

Preparation Time: Serving: Difficulty Level:

Ingredients

....
....
....
....
....
....

Steps for preparation

_____
_____
_____
_____
_____
_____
_____
_____

Recipe Name _____

Preparation Time: Serving: Difficulty Level:

Ingredients

....
....
....
....
....
....

Steps for preparation

_____
_____
_____
_____
_____
_____
_____
_____

Recipe Name _____

Preparation Time: Serving: Difficulty Level:

Ingredients

....
....
....
....
....
....

Steps for preparation

_____
_____
_____
_____
_____
_____
_____
_____
_____

Recipe Name _____

Preparation Time: Serving: Difficulty Level:

Ingredients

....
....
....
....
....
....

Steps for preparation

_____
_____
_____
_____
_____
_____
_____
_____

Recipe Name _____

Preparation Time: Serving: Difficulty Level:

Ingredients

....
....
....
....
....
....

Steps for preparation

_____
_____
_____
_____
_____
_____
_____
_____
_____

Recipe Name _____

Preparation Time: Serving: Difficulty Level:

Ingredients

....
....
....
....
....
....

Steps for preparation

_____
_____
_____
_____
_____
_____
_____
_____
_____

Printed in Great Britain
by Amazon